Sunset

LANDSCAPING WITH ORNAMENTAL GRASSES

BY FIONA GILSENAN AND THE EDITORS OF SUNSET BOOKS

SUNSET BOOKS · MENLO PARK, CALIFORNIA

GLORIOUS GRASSES

By incorporating ornamental grasses into your garden, you are doing more than choosing just another plant out of the many available. You are inviting nature into your landscape. With their naturalistic simplicity, grasses are the perfect plants for a new gardening sensibility, one that works in harmony with the earth rather than struggling against it.

Most grasses require little care—minimal fertilizer, occasional grooming, and just enough water to meet their needs. They are rarely subject to diseases, and they won't bring plagues of insects into your garden. If you choose wisely, even bamboos won't escape to wreak havoc in the neighbor's yard. But by choosing such undemanding plants, are you sacrificing color and interest in the garden?

The images in this book are proof that grasses bring with them not only simplicity but also variety and beauty. The many ways you can use grasses will probably surprise you—to create low-growing meadowlike lawns and dramatic mixed borders, to reshape your garden with tunnels and screens, or to fix a problem spot with a clever planting scheme. Simply put, gardening with grasses is fun.

For their invaluable help in producing this book, we would like to thank all the consultants who reviewed the text, and the gardeners and landscaping professionals who shared their wonderful gardens. For his vision and passion for ornamental grasses, we are especially grateful to John Greenlee.

SUNSET BOOKS

Vice President, General Manager: Richard A. Smeby
Vice President, Editorial Director: Bob Doyle
Production Director: Lory Day
Director of Operations: Rosann Sutherland
Art Director: Vasken Guiragossian

Staff for this book:

Sunset Books Senior Editor, Gardening: Marianne Lipanovich
Senior Editor: Tom Wilhite
Assistant Editor: Susan M. Guthrie
Copy Chief: Elissa Rabellino
Indexer: Erin Hartshorn
Photo Editor: Cynthia Del Fava
Production Coordinator: Danielle Javier
Contributing Writers: Stevie Daniels, Karen Fischer, Steven R. Lorton, Jim McCausland, Lauren Bonar Sweezey

Art Direction and Computer Production: Robin Weiss Graphic Design
Illustrators: Susan Carlson, Paulette Dennis, Rik Olson, Mimi Osborne, Erin O'Toole, Jenny Speckels, Ann Weiss Illustration

Cover: Photography and garden design by Lauren Springer. Border photograph by Charles Mann.

For additional copies of *Landscaping with Ornamental Grasses* or any other Sunset book, call 1-800-526-5111 or visit us at www.sunset.com.

PHOTOGRAPHERS:

Photographs are listed sequentially. For clarification, the following position indicators may be used: Top (T), Middle (M), Bottom (B); Left (L), Right (R).

Curtis Anderson: 117 BR. **Scott Atkinson:** 118 BR. **Max Badgeley/Temperate Bamboo Quarterly:** 120 TR. **Mark Bolton/The Garden Picture Library:** 28 T. **Marion Brenner:** 1; 3 ML; 10 TR; 25 BL; 33 BR; 35 MR; 38; 40 T; 45 BL; 48 BL; 51 BL; 53 TL; 54 B; 59 TL; 79 T; 84 TR; 88 TR; 89 BR; 104 L. **The Bridgeman Art Library International Ltd.:** 14 T. **David Cavagnaro:** 6 MR; 11 TL; 107 TR. **Walter Chandoha:** 56 TL, TR; 57 TL, TR. **Peter Christiansen:** 34 BL. **Claire Curran:** 119 MR. **Robin B. Cushman:** 6 BL; 7 ML; 8 BL; 52 BL; 75 TL; 100 BL. **Stevie Daniels:** 33 TL; 72 TR. **Janet Davis:** 110 BR. **Arnaud Descat/ Mise au Point:** 11 TR. **Alan & Linda Detrick:** 76 L; 109 BR. **Charlene Edwards:** 12 B, T. **Derek Fell:** 14 B; 15 BL; 18 BL; 47 TL; 101 BL. **Roger Foley:** 3 T; 4; 80 BL, BR; 85 BL; 86 B; 87 BL; 94 TR; 96 B; 97 BR. **Fiona Gilsenan:** 61 TR; 63 BR; 65 BR; 119 TR. **John Glover/The Garden Picture Library:** 34 TL; 92 BR. **Juliet Greene/The Garden Picture Library:** 64 BR; 104 ML. **John Greenlee:** 2; 7 TL; 9 TR; 12 M; 13 TL; 15 BR; 19 B; 21 ML; 22 BR; 23 TL; 24 T; 29 MR, BR; 31 TL, ML; 33 TR, BL; 35 TL; 41 M; 43 BL; 46 BR; 47 TR; 48 TR; 49 TL, BR; 54 T; 55 BL; 59 TM; 62 ALL; 70 MR; 74 TR; 76 R; 77 BR; 78 L; 82 TR; 92 BL; 100 TL; 101 BR; 108 BL; 110 TM, BL; 112 BR; 115 TR; 120 L; 121 BL. **Jamie Hadley:** 102 TL. **Mick Hales:** 80 T. **Acey Harper:** 112 TL. **Jerry Harpur:** 15 T; 18 BR; 26 M; 29 ML; 55 TR; 67 B; 70 BL; 83 TR; 93 BR; 101 TR. **Marcus Harpur:** 52 BR. **Phil Harvey:** 78 TR; 89 TR. **Marijke Heuff/The Garden Picture Library:** 42 T; 45 MR. **Saxon Holt:** 78 BL; 79 BL; 87 BR; 88 BR. **Sandra Ivany:** 27 BR. **Andrea Jones/The Garden Picture Library:** 7 BR. **Dency Kane:** 43 MR. **Andrew Lawson:** 10 BR; 44 T; 63 TL; 64 BL; 94 MR; 100 BR; 102 BR. **Randy Leffingwell:** 65 BL. **Janet Loughrey:** 88 BR. **Richard Maack:** 24 M; 42 BR; 65 T. **Kathryn MacDonald:** 106 TL, TR; 107 T; 108 TL, BR; 109 TR. **Allan Mandell:** 10 TL; 13 BL; 20 BR; 22 TR, 40 BR, BL; 51 TL, TR; 52 TL; 60 BR; 88 ML; 103 TR; 111 TR. **Charles Mann:** 3 TR; 7 T; 8 T; 9 TL, BR; 16; 18 ML; 20 T, BL; 21 TR; 22 BL; 23 MR, BR, BL; 24 BL; 25 TL; 30 B; 31 MR, 32 TL, 41 T; 42 BL; 43 TL, TR; 44 M; 45 BR; 46 BL, TR; 49 TR; 53 B; 58 ALL; 59 TR; 60 BL; 72 ML; 73 TR; 93 TL; 96 TR. **Chas McGrath:** 112 BL. **N. et P. Mioulane/Mise au Point:** 13 TR. **Terrence Moore:** 81 B; 89 L. **Kit Morris:** 36 ALL; 37 ALL; 86 TR. **Don Normark:** 110 TL. **Carol Ottesen:** 81 TR. **Jerry Pavia:** 11 BL, BR; 45 TR; 60 T; 61 B; 67 T; 75 ML; 84 BR; 87 TL; 103 TL. **Norman A. Plate:** 3 BL; 23 TR; 90 TR; 98; 103 TM, BR; 104 MR, BR; 105; 116 TL, ML; 118 TL; 119 ML. **Rob Proctor:** 103. **Sandra Lee Reha:** 121 BR. **Ian Reeves:** 114 TR; 116 BL1, BL2, BL3, BL4. **Howard Rice/The Garden Picture Library:** 102 TR. **Susan A. Roth:** 3 BR; 6 T; 8 BR; 19 TL; 50 T; 66; 67 M; 68; 70 ML; 75 TR; 77 TR; 91 TL, BR; 97 BL; 101 TL; 102 BL; 106 B. **David Salman/High Country Gardens:** 113 BL, BR. **Alec Scaresbrook/The Garden Picture Library:** 59 B. **Richard Shiell:** 77 L. **JS Sira/The Garden Picture Library:** 95. **Chad Slattery:** 70 TR. **Lauren Springer:** 19 TR; 34 TR, BR; 72 BR. **W.D.A. Stephens:** 115 BL. **Ron Sutherland/The Garden Picture Library:** 41 B. **Michael S. Thompson:** 21 BR; 25 BR; 49 BL; 53 TR; 55 TL; 63 BL; 64 BL; 82 BR; 84 ML; 91 BL; 94 BL; 100 TR. **James A. van Sweden:** 14 M. **Deidra Walpole:** 101 TM. **Peter O. Whiteley:** 78 BR. **Ros Wickham/ The Garden Picture Library:** 64 TR. **Tom Wilhite:** 79 BR. **Cynthia Woodyard:** 104 TR. **Steven Wooster/The Garden Picture Library:** 92 TR.

Contents

THE NATURE OF GRASSES

Grasses are rightly classified as a botanical group, but within that group is a world of versatility—both in and out of the garden. Towering bamboo provides vertical screening; Carex pansa can make a meadowlike lawn that rarely needs mowing; Briza maxima is an annual grass that quickly shoots up to 18 inches to fill gaps in the border; the many varieties of Miscanthus sinensis intermingle happily with shrubs and perennials on a slope. There are fragrant grasses, such as Japanese sweet flag (Acorus gramineus), and grasses suited to culinary purposes, such as edible bamboo shoots or savory vanilla grass. Many grasses make great subjects for floral arrangements, or can be fashioned into crafts or building projects. About the only things you can't do with grasses are grow them up an arbor or train them to a topiary.

It's generally said that grasses have succeeded as a group because of their adaptability. They have evolved to suit almost every environment and climate on earth, from high mountain meadows to deserts, bogs to prairies, shady woodlands to shifting sands. Gardeners are also the beneficiaries of this diversity, for as the following pages show, there are grasses suitable for pretty much any garden, in any situation, and in every climate zone.

This fall display in Kurt Bluemel's nursery in Maryland illustrates the variety of form and color of grasses grown for ornamental purposes.

ORIGIN OF THE SPECIES

Many of our most popular orna-mentals came from abroad. Perhaps the most ubiquitous horti-cultural grass species, Miscanthus, is native to Asia; phormiums come from New Zealand; and many other familiar garden species grasses originated in milder Euro-pean climates. But North America also boasts an impressive array of habitats, and some of our finest garden specimens trace their ori-gins to the central prairies, Eastern woodlands, or Western mountain ranges.

The vast North American prairies contain several different ecosystems. The Great Plains short-grass prairies are similar to Asian steppes, with native buf-falo grass and blue grama. This short-grass prairie with sunflowers is in the Badlands of South Dakota. The once-endless tall-grass prairie—now the agri-cultural corn belt—has rich soil and native species that include big bluestem, Indian rice grass, and switch grass. Although many of the original prairies have been long-since plowed under or paved over, many gardeners in the heartland are restoring and rejuvenating these ecosystems for both horticultural and ecological purposes.

Coastal saltwater marshes call to mind sleepy estu-aries lined with rippling reeds and lapping waves. Unlike many other ecosystems, they retain their grass-dominated character, as long as invasive species are not introduced. This peaceful waterway is in Point Reyes, California.

Although the term "savanna" conjures up the expanses of Africa, North America has its own versions. Found where woodlands and prairies meet, savannas are essentially open grass-lands with scattered trees. This oak savanna in Eugene, Oregon, is studded with native camass *(Camassia)* in spring.

Alpine meadows aren't only found in Switzerland. America has its own share of wildflower-strewn grasslands located at high altitudes. The Rocky Mountains, naturally, have some spectacular natural meadows, but the inland ranges of California and Nevada also feature many pristine sites such as this one near Lake Tahoe.

The drier areas of the West contain mixed-grass prairie, with such natives as little bluestem, June grass, needle grass, and wheatgrass. In the Sonoran desert, giant sacaton *(Sporobolus wrightii)* is found amid wildflowers, cactus, and other desert plants.

From eastern woodlands to Rocky Mountain pine forests, grasses form much of the understory. Shade tolerant and often moisture loving, cultivated versions of these grasses often feature striking variegation or chartreuse hues that draw the eye amid the shadows.

Beach grass stabilizes sandy soil, preventing dunes from eroding (see page 70). Native American beach grass, *Ammophila breviligulata,* is found in the Northeast and along the shores of the Great Lakes. Its European counterpart, *Ammophila arenaria* (shown here), is now widespread through much of the coastal South and West, having displaced other native dune grasses.

THE "REAL" GRASSES

What makes a grass a grass? Membership in the Poaceae family, primarily. But grasses are unlike other garden plants in several ways. One distinguishing feature is their growth habit: Grasses grow upward from the base of the leaf or the shoot, which means that even if cut, burned, or eaten, the plant can regrow. True grasses generally have extensive root systems, which form a thick matrix of growth. And the "fruit" of most grasses is what we think of as seeds or grains.

Grasses may be either perennial or annual, and these definitions vary from one climate to another. A grass that might be considered an evergreen perennial in a warm climate, for instance, would be one that retains its color throughout the seasons. In a colder climate, however, that same plant might die to the ground each winter only to regrow in spring. In a still harsher climate, the plant may simply die back altogether in response to freezing temperatures. An annual grass is one that completes its growth cycle in a single year, and there are relatively few of these in garden culture.

Other plants we consider grass-like are those that resemble grasses in their growth habits (see pages 10–11). They are often some of the best companions for interplanting with grasses, or they can be used in similar ways in the garden.

Bamboos are true grasses, but they are all rhizomatous and have hollow woody *culms* (also called stems or canes) and erratic flowering schedules. As with other grasses, different types have different growth habits. Clumpers spread more slowly, with a denser, noninvasive habit. Unless you have a very large property, you will have to control the growth of running bamboos, which practically define the word "invasive." Their rhizomes grow parallel to the soil surface, sending up new canes along the way—often ducking under concrete paths, walls, and other obstacles. Control is possible, however, with physical restraints or other barriers (see page 115). Shown here are (at left) running black bamboo *(Phyllostachys nigra)* and clumping *Fargesia nitida* (right).

Many grasses—tall and short— are referred to as *clumping, bunching,* or *tussock grasses*. These plants send out side shoots called *tillers* and form discrete mounds rather than a solid mat. You don't have to worry about these types spreading invasively into adjoining areas, and their growth habit makes them suitable for a range of situations, from perennial borders to natural lawns. Shown here is clumping deer grass *(Muhlenbergia rigens)*.

Grasses are also distinguished from other garden plants by their flowers, which are pollinated by wind and therefore have not evolved the showy colors and shapes of those dependent on insects for pollination. Shown here are the tiny flowers of Indian grass *(Sorghastrum nutans)*.

Many perennial grasses native to cool temperate climates have rhizomes or stolons that spread out to form a dense mat, rapidly covering ground without producing seeds. These are the grasses typically used for turf lawns. Under some circumstances, running grasses can become invasive.

HOT OR COLD?

Select grasses for your garden based on their preferred growth habit in your area. Cool-season grasses start growing in early spring, flower in spring and summer, then stop growing in hot summer temperatures. They may revive in fall but are completely dormant in winter. Warm-season grasses grow in the heat of summer, when they produce long-lasting, showy seed heads. Whether a grass is a cool- or a warm-season grower is not a definite indication of its hardiness (its ability to withstand cold winter temperatures). Some that thrive in moderate temperatures cannot tolerate excess heat. And yet others require a period of winter chill in order to grow their best. You'll find more information on hardiness and climate throughout this book, but your best guide to the suitability of plants for your area is a knowledgeable local nurseryman or Cooperative Extension agent.

Cool-season grower *Calamagrostis × acutiflora* 'Karl Foerster' (top) can't tolerate extreme heat; tender *Pennisetum setaceum* 'Rubrum' (below) is killed by winter frost.

Botany students remember that "sedges have edges," meaning that members of the *Carex* family *(Cyperaceae)* have solid, triangular stems as opposed to the hollow, cylindrical stems of true grasses. But what gardeners need to know is that sedges are versatile and generally evergreen, and they have spiky flower heads. Many sedges are woodland plants and need plenty of moisture, but others are drought tolerant and make excellent border plants or natural lawns (see pages 28–31).

New Zealand is the home of the only two known species of phormium, *P. tenax* and *P. cookianum,* thus the common name New Zealand flax. Widely used as specimens and impressive accents, phormium cultivars are available in colors that range from green to fiery red (rear) or bronze, and from dwarf to truly massive types. Silver-leafed *Astelia* (foreground) resembles a phormium but differs in coloration and flower form. If you have the space, either plant can be truly stunning in masses.

You might want to experiment with plants that have straplike leaves, such as lilies, daylilies, montbretia, and fairy wand (right). Not only does their foliage resemble the clumping stems of grasses, but they provide a bonus in the form of their colorful and varied flowers.

The *Juncaceae* and *Cyperaceae* families resemble grasses in appearance and growth habit, spreading widely from the base. Akin to them are cattails, which have a familiar thickened flower head. All the plants of these families are moisture lovers, thriving in standing water or well-irrigated soil.

Recently introduced into North American nurseries and gardens, restios are native to Australia and the cape region of South Africa. These plants resemble reeds and rushes, with upright stems tipped with chocolate brown flowers. Although *Chondropetalum* and *Elegia* are the only two genera currently widely available, you can expect to see more restios entering the garden market in the future. Shown here is the Australian native *Restio tetraphyllum*.

Many succulent plants resemble grasses in overall form and in their water and fertilizer needs, which are minimal. With their water-retentive stems or roots and showy flowers, though, succulents are horticulturally quite removed from the grass family. Not only do succulents and grasses mingle well in desert-themed gardens, where their cultural requirements are few, but many also make striking container specimens, much like the larger grasses (see pages 100–105).

Popular as a turf-grass substitute, low-growing, straplike *Ophiopogon* and closely related *Liriope* form evergreen clumps that can be tucked along paths or between flower beds and lawns, or mixed with groupings of boulders or stepping-stones. Most need regular watering and protection from harshest sunlight. Flowers are generally white or blue, and some types produce tiny but showy berries.

FROM HARDWORKING TO HORTICULTURAL

Grasses have been appreciated for their utility far longer than for their beauty. Many cultures have depended on members of the grass family in order to maintain or improve their living standards. References to grain and cereal crops, grasses as building materials, and pastureland grasses can be found throughout recorded history.

In North America, native peoples relied on agricultural crops such as corn in the Southwest, and forage grasses, which nourished buffalo and other grazing animals, in the Midwest. European settlers who first came to New England brought cattle from Europe, and cattle need to graze. The settlers began to import European forage grasses and in the process unintentionally introduced many more species. The arrival of these more aggressive foreign species changed the landscape of the continent in many ways.

The Great Plains were developed mostly as grazing land for cattle. Other prairie lands were planted over with corn, wheat, barley, and similar crops—most introduced or developed in nonnative habitats.

Although generations of writers have extolled the beauty of waving fields of grass, it's only recently that the idea of grasses as ornamental garden plants has become widespread, encouraged not only by their beauty but also by their undemanding character in the garden.

Just as grasses have flowers, they also have fruits—although not what we generally think of tossing into a fruit salad. These include such agricultural staples as wheat, barley, corn, and oats. *Zizania,* better known as rice, is one of the essential components of the world's food supply, providing basic sustenance for millions of people.

In the West, the farming of cereal grasses has led to such familiar sights as fields of cropland (below) and grain elevators (left).

The thick, jointed stems of the Mediter-ranean native *Arundo donax* (giant reed) resemble bamboo and have been used in structures for many years. It is seen here, for example, as plant supports in northern Italy. The plant is also the source of reeds for flutes and other wind instruments, and it is still cultivated for this purpose in southern France. In Southern California, on the other hand, the giant reed has become a pest plant in riverbeds and other moist habitats.

One of the predominant products that fueled Euro-American trade through the last few centuries, sugar cane *(Saccharum officinarum)* is a tropical plant grown on vast plantations throughout the Caribbean, the West Indies, and other tropical regions. These sugar cane fields are in Maui, Hawaii.

Bamboo is native to moist temperate forests in Asia, Africa, and South America. References to the cultivation of bamboo stretch back for centuries in Asia, where bamboo has held both ornamental and utilitarian value— as a building material, in indoor and outdoor decor, and as edible plants. At one time in North America various invasive species were planted in home gardens, earning the entire plant family an unsavory reputation as unstoppable weeds—a reputation bamboo has outgrown.

INTO THE GARDEN

Grasses were cultivated in horticulture very much later than in agriculture, but they have been used in gardens longer than you might suppose. Medieval texts speak of "flowery meads," wildflower-dotted grassy meadows found around stately homes; these were precursors not only of turf lawns but also of natural lawns and meadows. By the late 1800s, several dozen grasses were considered fine subjects for traditional borders and transitional areas of the garden, and were promoted by such legendary gardeners as William Robinson and Gertrude Jekyll. (In his seminal 1883 book, The English Flower Garden, *Robinson describes the virtues of such garden-worthy grasses as blue lyme grass* (Leymus arenarius), Panicum *species, pennisetums, and feather grass* (Stipa).

The first large-scale introduction of grass was in the form of lawns in 18th-century Europe, especially in France and England. They remained a status symbol, requiring large numbers of workers with scythes or sheep to keep them trimmed. When the lawnmower was invented in the 1800s, it made ownership of a lawn possible for the less wealthy. In the United States, the postwar suburban boom is credited with taking the lawn beyond mainstream to the almost iconic status it currently enjoys.

The poetic-sounding flowery mead is depicted in artworks of the 16th and 17th centuries, including the famous Unicorn Tapestries now housed in the Cloisters in New York. They are described as idyllic seminatural havens, sweet smelling and full of flowers, in which to picnic and strum lutes.

As ornamentals, grasses truly came into their own in the second half of the 20th century. The German nurseryman Karl Foerster is generally credited with introducing the gardening public to the uses of grasses for year-round plantings. His 1950 book, *The Uses of Grasses and Ferns in the Garden,* was one of the first to treat grasses as a prominent ornamental group.

Influenced by Foerster was Kurt Bluemel, who, along with Wolfgang Oehme, established a nursery trade in grasses in the United States. With his design partner, James van Sweden, Oehme developed a signature style of grass plantings inspired by the American prairies. The "New American" style of garden design features grasses planted in great blocks and sweeps, layered with natural companions such as rudbeckia, coneflower, and other American native plants. Shown here is a grassy nook in Kurt Bluemel's garden.

In the Netherlands, Piet Oudolf has a highly recognizable style, consisting of the use of lush, sweeping borders that combine perennials and grasses.

One of the pioneers of garden design in the Americas was the Brazilian Roberto Burle Marx, who studied in Germany and also was influenced by Foerster. His often large-scale designs in South American private and public gardens were characterized by mass curvilinear grass plantings, multi-colored lawns, and the use of exotic tropical plants. This garden is the Monteiro residence in Petropolis, Rio de Janeiro, Brazil.

In addition to the work of East Coast innovators such as Oehme and Van Sweden, there are other channels through which grasses are finding their way into plantings. In the Midwest, prairie restoration and meadow gardens are becoming more popular as gardeners come to understand how to adapt these ecosystems for home landscapes. Shown here is the garden at Neil Diboll's residence in Wisconsin. Similarly, in the West, a desire for low maintenance and a less rigid aesthetic have inspired designers and nursery experts to develop nonthirsty lawns and to integrate grasses and grasslike plants into garden designs that range from formal to casual.

A NOTE ON NATIVES

Does gardening with grasses mean "going native"? Not necessarily. Although some gardeners favor grasses that are indigenous to their geographic regions, many others employ a more relaxed standard when choosing plants. The key is to find plants whose cultural demands match the conditions in your garden. This might mean a garden that features natives, but it easily might also be a garden with plants drawn from similar environments around the globe. Keep in mind that a truly dedicated gardener can grow almost any plant by providing the right combination of shelter, water, soil, and food. But if you prefer a garden that doesn't have to be on life support, it's much simpler to put your efforts into finding the right plant for the right spot.

THE
LOWDOWN

We are most used to seeing grass grown in one way—as lawn. And because turf grasses are always closely cropped, we think of grass as one continuous expanse of green. Who considers each individual grass plant? Probably no one did until the attention-grabbing Miscanthus, Calamagrostis, *and* Pennisetum *species began appearing in home and commercial landscapes across the country. This new perspective liberated grasses from their single-minded use as turf and opened a new world of possibilities. Now, not only are the low-growing grasses intriguing alternatives to traditional lawns, but they also hold their own as edgings, borders, and ground covers.*

By low growers, we mean those grasses that range from the 5-inch fine-leafed Festuca *species—such as red fescue and sheep fescue—and the grasslike* Carex *species to the 18-inch blue oat grass (*Helictotrichon sempervirens) *and* Sesleria autumnalis. *A key characteristic of these grasses is that most (but not all) of them are bunching types. They grow in clumps as opposed to spreading (as do conventional turf grasses), which means you have a choice: You can either plant them close together to fully cover an area, or space them farther apart and then interplant companionable perennials, bulbs, or wildflowers.*

Lindheimer's muhly *(Muhlenbergia lindheimeri)* combined with African daisy *(Dimorphotheca sinuata)* forms a meadow of year-round color. Several *Muhlenbergia* species form clumps under 2 feet tall, although the flower stalks may be taller. Design: Julia Berman.

STEPPING OUT

To fill in the edges of a patio or add interest between paving stones, select the lowest-growing (3 to 6 inches) and finest-textured grasses and sedges. These plants visually soften the edges of a hard masonry surface and add color, but you must be sure the surface is as flat as possible for foot traffic.

In some climates, a drought-tolerant species might survive with no supplemental watering, but in most cases, the hot sun reflected off stone can quickly dry out the surrounding soil and kill the plants. So if you are putting in a new patio, space the pavers far enough to allow room for drip irrigation tubing between them. Or if you have a sprinkler system, set it to run at night, when the irrigation water is least likely to evaporate and the slick paving stones won't cause anyone to slip.

Think of safety when it comes to the plants' height as well. If you select a low-growing species to plant between the pavers, you won't need to mow at all. But a taller one will need occasional mowing to keep the surface relatively smooth.

With geometric precision, rows of *Sesleria caerulea* fit between square pavers in this Vancouver Island garden. The leaves are bluish on top with dark green undersides, which gives the plant a two-tone look. Because its native habitats are often alkaline or rocky soils, it is well suited to the rigors of a concrete patio—but it must have sufficient moisture.

Less than 4 inches tall, *Carex firma* 'Variegata' is well suited to rock gardens and gravel surfaces.

Neither the paving nor the plantings are uniform on this patio, and it makes for an exuberant mix of color and texture. In the patchwork openings between broken concrete and brick grow a variety of grasses and ground covers, including sedges, New Zealand flax, and feather grass.

The low-growing habit of Catlin sedge *(Carex texensis)* makes it ideal for using between stones, but its fine texture belies its toughness. This evergreen grows no taller than 3 to 4 inches, and it can be used in sun or shade even where there is likely to be significant foot traffic.

The unusual dark purple blooms of this fountain grass *(Pennisetum alopecuroides* 'Moudry') are a stunning complement to the dark and light gray tones of the irregularly shaped stones in the pathway. As the foliage grows, its mounding form reaches about 2 feet in height, which also defines and softens the edge of the path.

Distinctive and unique among grasses, bamboo muhly *(Muh-lenbergia dumosa)* has feathery bamboolike bright green foliage. Although it grows up to 4 feet, its draping habit can make it suitable as an edging plant. Native to Arizona, it won't survive cold winters but can be placed, as here, in a tender border lining a wood-chip path. Its companions are feathertop *(Pennisetum villosum* 'Feathertop') and annual coleus.

LOWEST OF THE LOW (UNDER 1 FOOT)

Acorus gramineus JAPANESE SWEET FLAG
Agrostis canina 'Silver Needles'
A. pallens BENT GRASS
Andropogon ternarius SPLIT-BEARD BROOM SEDGE
A. virginicus BROOM SEDGE
Anthoxanthum odoratum SWEET VERNAL GRASS
Aristida purpurea PURPLE THREE-AWN
Arrhenatherum elatius bulbosum 'Variegatum'
  STRIPED BULBOUS OAT GRASS
Bouteloua gracilis BLUE GRAMA
Buchloe dactyloides BUFFALO GRASS
Carex caryophyllea 'The Beatles' MOP-HEADED
  SEDGE
C. pansa CALIFORNIA MEADOW SEDGE
C. pensylvanica PENNSYLVANIA SEDGE
C. perdentata TEXAS MEADOW SEDGE
C. senta BALTIMORE SEDGE
C. texensis CATLIN SEDGE
C. tumulicola BERKELEY SEDGE
Danthonia californica CALIFORNIA OAT GRASS
D. spicata POVERTY OAT GRASS
Festuca idahoensis IDAHO FESCUE
F. rubra RED FESCUE
Sesleria caerulea BLUE MOOR GRASS

Not only does *Acorus gramineus* 'Ogon' respond well to moist soil, forming dense clumps of bright buttery color in shady spots, but it is also wonderfully fragrant when crushed. Here it provides a brilliant underpinning for a metal sculpture, and mounds politely over the edge of a gravel path.

One of the most interesting features of the grasses is their flower heads. The row of fountain grass *(Pennisetum alopecuroides)* has been positioned along this walkway to catch the late-afternoon sun. In this special light, the fuzzy blooms seem to glow, which beautifully complements the ruddy texture of the pathway.

Grasses are the central feature in the borders lining this walkway in a garden designed by Julia Berman. The foreground features blue oat grass *(Helictotrichon sempervirens)* with Mexican feather grass *(Nassella tenuissima)* behind. *Miscanthus* species provide a taller contrast in the back of the bed, on the right. Creeping thyme is used between the stepping-stones.

Bronze-brown and flowing, the foliage of New Zealand hair sedge *(Carex comans)* makes a fine spiller along a pathway. The color picks up tones in the gravel, creating a smooth transition of shades from the path to the background greens.

The draping habit of certain low-growing grasses makes them an attractive choice for use along the edges of steps, paths, and patios. Both *Acorus gramineus* 'Ogon' and *Hakonechloa macra* 'Aureola' have brillant yellow foliage, but they must be placed in a semishady spot in moist, well-drained soil that doesn't dry out. The glowing border of this perennial bed designed by Bob Clark complements the variegated miscanthus behind, especially viewed against the taller broad-leafed perennials.

Lower-growing fescues line a path leading to a small bridge. The drama of the approach to this focal point is heightened by using gradually taller plants. Purple needle grass *(Nassella pulchra)*, native to California, sends up long purplish seed stems in late winter, which turn silver as they age.

While creeping herbs snake along the cracks between these stepping-stones, taller perennials and grasses line the walk. Rust-colored leather leaf sedge *(Carex buchananii)* is planted with pink tickseed *(Coreopsis rosea)* for a brown-gold combination that stands out against the rosy-colored paving stones. In the background rise tall *Miscanthus* species and kniphofia.

FILLING IN

Many low-growing clumping grasses make excellent edging plants for perennial beds; surrounds for features such as specimen trees, lights, or birdhouses; or simply naturalistic plantings. For the most dramatic appearance, choose just one species for edging around a particular bed. Space the plants so that they'll touch each other or mingle with surrounding plants when they have reached their mature size.

Japanese forest grass *(Hakonechloa macra* 'Aureola') has weeping, bamboolike foliage that reaches about 1 to 3 feet. It loves light shade, and spreads slowly by rhizomes to create a soft mound. The clumps are ideal for planting beneath trees, bamboo, or sculptural stakes, as shown here.

Blue fescue *(Festuca glauca)* forms orderly mounds about 6 inches tall. It is best suited for informal arrangements such as this blue-and-rose combination with cheddar pinks *(Dianthus gratianopolitanus).*

Any of the low-growing, clumping grasses or sedges can be used to fill in the foreground of a perennial bed. Because of its distinctive color, Japanese blood grass *(Imperata cylindrica* 'Rubra') makes an interesting contrast to a predominantly green area. And because it spreads slowly by rhizomes, it is best used as a specimen or in groups as a filler.

Use a low to medium-height bunching grass that can tolerate part shade to fill in beds around a small tree. Plants that could pick up the gold accents of this tree include *Luzula* species, feather grass, wild oats *(Chasmanthium latifolium)*, blue moor grass *(Sesleria caerulea),* and *Carex* species.

Low-growing grasses such as red fescue *(Festuca rubra)* and Berkeley sedge *(Carex tumulicola)* flow like a bumpy sea around boulders in this Japanese-style garden. Jana Ruzicka designed the garden, which is in Laguna Beach, California, adding spiky yuccas and bamboo for the shadow patterns they make on the plain walls.

In a border in the garden of Ann Mehafy, Mexican feather grass and blue fescue *(Festuca glauca)* are combined with *Persicaria amplexicaule* 'Firetail', whose reddish brown flower spikes blend beautifully with the foliage of the feather grass.

Striped bulbous oat grass *(Arrhenatherum elatius bulbosum* 'Variegatum'), which reaches only 10 inches in height, is an excellent edging plant. It spreads slowly by producing new plants from bulbs at the base. In hot climates, plant it in partial shade. Here it is mingled with maiden pinks *(Dianthus deltoides),* which form mats of dark green grasslike foliage.

This combination of different heights and colors was put together by designer Bob Clark. It includes ribbon grass *(Phalaris arundinacea* 'Picta') in front, with zebra grass *(Miscanthus sinensis* 'Zebrinus') and New Zealand flax behind.

SPREADING OUT

For an exuberant, natural look, plant a large area with randomly spaced mounding clumps of one, two, or three grass species interspersed with stones or low-growing perennials. Keep in mind that grasses are most effective when blended with broad-leafed plants such as certain bulbs, perennials, or small shrubs. And their effect is most striking when they can be viewed against a background. Look at the site. Is there a group of shrubs, a tree, or a fence? When you install the plants, you can space them closely for quick cover and move some later when they begin to crowd each other. Or plant them far enough apart to allow each one room to reach mature size, and apply mulch or large stones between them. Most grasses will fill in quickly.

Combine cool-season and warm-season grasses with evergreen sedges *(Carex* species) to create a low planting with year-round interest. The light beige fluffy blooms of fountain grass *(Pennisetum* species) are set off by their medium green foliage. The red leaves of Japanese blood grass *(Imperata cylindrica* 'Rubra') in the foreground and a sedge between the fountain grass clumps provide even more variation in color, height, and texture.

A low clumping grass forms a broad sweep across a slope behind this palo verde *(Cercidium).* In the foreground are desert marigolds *(Baileya multiradiata).*

In this naturalistic Albuquerque garden, blue grama *(Bouteloua gracilis)* is left unmowed. The clumping grass is interspersed with Shirley poppies and gray-leafed native white sage *(Artemesia ludoviciana).* Design: Daniel Forrest.

The clumping habit of many grasses provides an excellent palette for blending in low-growing perennials for color and interest. Here, Mexican feather grass is combined with twinspur *(Diascia)* and purple verbena, which bloom from spring through summer.

This meadowlike landscape was created with a mass planting of Mexican feather grass. The blue blooms of lavender and white *Centranthus ruber* 'Albus' are interspersed to serve as subtle punctuation marks against the golden grass. The garden was designed by Ron Lutsko.

GRASSES FOR MASSES

Acorus gramineus JAPANESE SWEET FLAG
Anthoxanthum odoratum SWEET VERNAL GRASS
Bouteloua curtipendula SIDE-OATS GRAMA
B. gracilis BLUE GRAMA
Buchloe dactyloides BUFFALO GRASS
Calamagrostis foliosa MENDOCINO REED GRASS
Deschampsia cespitosa TUFTED HAIR GRASS
Festuca rubra RED FESCUE
F. rubra trichophylla CREEPING RED FESCUE
F. tenuifolia FINE-LEAFED FESCUE
Helictotrichon sempervirens BLUE OAT GRASS
Holcus mollis 'Albovariegatus' VARIEGATED
  CREEPING SOFT GRASS
Nassella tenuissima MEXICAN FEATHER GRASS
Pennisetum species (some)
Sesleria species
Sporobolus heterolepis PRAIRIE DROPSEED

MADE FOR SHADE

Acorus gramineus JAPANESE SWEET FLAG
Carex elata 'Aurea' BOWLES' GOLDEN SEDGE
C. comans NEW ZEALAND HAIR SEDGE
C. morrowii expallida SILVER VARIEGATED
  JAPANESE SEDGE
Deschampsia (PART SHADE)
Luzula pilosa HAIRY WOODRUSH
L. purpurea PURPLE WOODRUSH
Sesleria species (PART SHADE)

This dazzling scene shows how beautifully a collection of mixed sedges fills in a large area. This combination includes leather leaf sedge *(Carex buchananii)*, *C. lucida*, orange New Zealand sedge *(C. testacea)*, and *C. trifida*.

THE LAWN

How did lawns come to be so ubiquitous in our landscapes? They first appeared in France in the late 18th century. The word "lawn" derives from the archaic French word *laund,* which in its earliest form referred to an open space between woods, and later, by about the 16th century, to a portion of a garden or pleasure ground covered with grass and kept closely cropped. The earliest lawns were planted with large patches of sod dug from naturally occurring meadows.

By the mid-1800s, areas were sometimes seeded with specific grass varieties. Species lists in old English garden books include fescues, bluegrass, ryegrass, and clover. These grass tracts were "mowed" by hand using scythes. Then, around 1830, an English engineer named Edwin Budding invented a machine to shear grass. The firm Ransomes, of Ipswich, England, introduced a gasoline-powered mower in 1902.

In the United States, the practice of mowing a grassy area around the home developed in the late 1800s as the population spread from the cities into single-family homes in the suburbs. Lawn grasses were imported from Europe. Andrew Jackson Downing, a landscape architect, and one of his students, Frank Scott, promoted the lawn as an essential visual foil or foreground for clusters of trees and shrubs. Scott went so far as to claim that every person had a "moral obligation" to maintain a well-kept lawn. Sears catalogs of the time reflect the increase of lawns with listings for lawnmowers, hoses, dandelion pullers, turf edgers, and lawn rollers.

Congress approved the first funding for turf grass research in 1901. But even though the early funding was for investigating both native and foreign species, the industry developed completely around nonnative grass species. In 1920, the U.S. Department of Agriculture, under heavy lobbying from the U.S. Golf Association, adopted a program to find grass species that were suitable for golf greens and fairways. It was looking for the best vegetative strains of creeping bent grass for golf greens and observing how other grass species, including Kentucky bluegrass and Bermuda grass, held up under the strain of heavy golf playing. Eventually most of the state agricultural universities developed turf-research

Beautifully manicured, stripe-mowed, and rolled perfectly flat, this English lawn represents the ultimate ideal for turf lovers—the croquet pitch. But in most American gardens, such a lawn can result only from tremendous labor, plentiful irrigation, and supplementary chemical assistance.

programs. Now we've discovered that foreign species are not well adapted and need large amounts of herbicides, pesticides, fertilizer, and water to keep them thriving. For many researchers and for home gardeners, the pendulum seems to be swinging away from these imports.

A CHANGE OF PERSPECTIVE

In 1910, only 23 percent of the American population lived in suburbs, which became symbolized by rows of single-family residences surrounded by mown lawns. By 1980 this had risen to 60 percent, and nearly two-thirds of the nation's residences were single-family homes. The lawn had become an entrenched part of the social fabric of American culture. But by the late 1980s, water shortages caused by drought, and other environmental concerns such as runoff of synthetic fertilizers and pesticides used to keep turf grass green and weed free, spurred a movement to find alternatives to the lawn.

Not only are there environmental concerns, but gardeners are less eager to spend their weekends cutting the grass and are looking for low-maintenance gardening solutions. At the same time, a new landscaping aesthetic has slowly been taking hold across the country—a desire for naturalistic, less formal gardens that echo the surrounding landscape and include native and well-adapted plants. In place of ripping up the lawn and paving over such a treasured part of our gardens, a trend is developing to use grasses that are better suited to particular eco-regions. The result is a new, and better, kind of lawn.

THE NEW LAWN

Imagine a feathery, emerald green lawn that needs watering only once a week and requires just two mowings a year. It may sound futuristic, but 'Rana Creek' fescue—a variety of a California native perennial bunchgrass—is available now.

In the wild, this grass grows and turns green when fall rains come, and stays green until late spring when dry weather drives it into dormancy. But in gardens in Monterey, California, it's given supplemental water once a week during the dry season, and remains green all year long. Mowing this grass is easy, too. It can be cut once in February or March and then again when it's dormant, just before rains start. Between mowings, it can grow 1 foot tall.

After the first year, fertilize 'Rana Creek' fescue in fall with an organic (urea-based) nitrogen fertilizer that releases in cool temperatures. (Note that not all natural lawn grasses tolerate fertilizing.) To find similar low-care turf grass substitutes for your area, read the information on the following pages and check the "Sources" list on pages 126 to 127. You can also call your local Cooperative Extension Office, or contact a local landscaping company or nursery that specializes in drought-resistant, native, or low-maintenance garden plants.

Landscape designer Michelle Comeau discovered the charms of 'Rana Creek' fescue on a trip to a local nursery.

You can transform most of your lawn into a natural meadowlike planting and keep a wide path (up to 4 feet) of maintained turf through the middle. Such an arrangement offers the best of both worlds—a soft, grassy area for playing or sitting, and also the natural, lower-maintenance meadow area that attracts birds and butterflies and provides an interesting display throughout the year.

NATURAL LAWN ALTERNATIVES

A so-called natural lawn takes its cues from the landscape. It may be planted with a grass species that is not native to the area but is nevertheless well adapted to the particular climate and soil type. You rarely need to fertilize a natural lawn or treat it with herbicides or pesticides. And the only time you need to water most natural lawns is when you put in the new plants—then you must irrigate regularly until they become established.

Some people think a natural lawn just means that you simply stop mowing your existing turf grass. But if you inherited a traditional lawn planted with a grass type that depends on regular applications of fertilizer, herbicides, pesticides, and water to maintain its appearance, such neglect will usually lead to a patch of weeds. To convert an existing lawn into a more natural planting, you'll need to continue mowing, if less often, and begin replacing small areas of the declining ill-suited turf grass with native or well-adapted species or ground covers.

However, even if you don't replant your lawn with native or other ornamental grasses, you can manage it differently for a more natural look. Plant low-growing flowering perennials in clusters here and there, and small spring-blooming bulbs such as *Chionodoxa,* blue squill *(Scilla siberica),* spring star flower *(Ipheion uniflorum),* and dwarf iris *(Iris verna).* Mow less often, and set the blade higher, about 4 inches, so that you can mow over the other plants without damaging the foliage.

Some creeping perennials to consider are pussy toes *(Antennaria),* African daisy *(Arctotis, Dimorphotheca,* or *Osteospermum),* English daisy *(Bellis perennis),* violets *(Viola*

species), baby blue eyes *(Nemophila menziesii),* sweet Dutch clover, blue star creeper *(Laurentia fluviatilis)* (in warmer areas), and snow-in-summer *(Cerastium tomentosum).*

If planting from scratch, you can create a meadowlike natural lawn by filling an area with a combination that includes one or two grass species, a mounding perennial, and some flowering perennials. In the West, such a lawn could include red fescue *(Festuca rubra),* coreopsis, and bearberry *(Arctostaphylos uva-ursi),* or deer grass *(Muhlenbergia rigens),* Mendocino reed grass *(Calamagrostis foliosa),* seaside daisy *(Erigeron glaucus),* golden aster *(Chrysopsis villosa),* and California poppies.

Another possible combination suitable mainly for the Southeast, is little bluestem, tickle grass *(Agrostis scabra),* blanket flower *(Gaillardia aristata),* lance-leafed coreopsis *(Coreopsis lanceolata),* and Mexican evening primrose *(Oenothera speciosa).* If you live in the Southwest, you can try a mixture of blue grama, buffalo grass, and purple three-awn *(Aristida purpurea),* with a combination of sand verbena *(Abronia fragrans),* desert marigold *(Baileya multiradiata),* wine cup *(Callirhoe involucrata),* and perky Sue *(Tetraneuris argentea).*

GRASSLIKE GROUND COVERS

When you want a low-growing, grassy look in areas not used for playing or sitting, consider a massed planting of a grasslike ground cover. The plants in this interesting group share characteristics that make them ideal for this use. They are evergreen, they form a dense cover that keeps down weeds, and many can handle a range of light conditions from sun to part shade.

For the most economical approach, place plants with sufficient distance between them so that each has room to reach mature size, then cover the empty space with mulch the first year or two to prevent weeds from encroaching. If you want a full cover quickly, you can space the plants more closely, but you will need to move some later as they begin to crowd each other.

Although bamboo does belong to the grass family, it can also be considered as a ground cover because it has such a different appearance from that of most grasses. Long, narrow, straplike leaves line the stems, most of which range in height from 3 to 6 feet or more. The lowest-growing one is pygmy bamboo. Grasslike *Carex* species are discussed on the following pages.

Use mondo grass *(Ophiopogon japonicus)* to fill in large areas where you want a grasslike appearance but not a lawn. This plant is native to Asia and can be used in warmer zones in sun or shade—it's a popular choice in the Southeast. It is a sod-forming, spreading plant that grows in clumps 8 to 16 inches high and is usually dark green. *O. planiscapus* 'Nigrescens' (or 'Arabicus') has deep purple-black leaves. If the plants look shabby in spring, just mow before new growth begins.

Big blue lily turf *(Liriope muscari)* is well adapted to most parts of the United States. It can be used in full sun to deep shade and tolerates prolonged dry spells. In the South and West it needs afternoon shade and is not suitable at all for desert areas. In colder parts of the country, the leaves may look spent by winter's end and require mowing before new growth begins.

Japanese sweet flag *(Acorus gramineus)* is also native to Asia and works well in warmer parts of the United States. An evergreen plant with glossy green grasslike foliage, it grows 6 to 10 inches tall and will take light traffic. The plants spread slowly by rhizomes and can be used in sun or light shade but must have consistent moisture.

Natural Lawn Alternatives **29**

USING NATIVES FOR LAWNS

Choosing a native grass or group of grasses suited to the particular region in which you live may be the best way to create a natural lawn. But a native planting doesn't have to be a 3-foot-high meadow. Horticulturalists and landscape designers have identified several dozen native species that will work successfully for a lawn-type planting, many of them less than a foot tall. There may be more possibilities among the 1,000 indigenous grass species, but for now these are the only ones available to consumers.

A number of these species are naturally low-growing (5 to 6 inches), which means they can be left unmowed if desired. Others grow somewhat taller and send up attractive seed-bearing stems. If you prefer a smoother appearance, both the short and tall types can be cut once or twice during the growing season. If you intend to create a habitat for small mammals, ground-nesting birds, and other wildlife, it is important to avoid cutting during nesting times; very early spring or late fall are the best times to mow.

Native grasses, like nonnatives, are either cool-season or warm-season types (see page 9). If you are planting seed, cool-season types do best when sown in fall, warm-season ones in late spring when the soil has warmed up. If you are adding native wild-flowers to the lawn, the best method is to sow the seeds and let the grass become established in the first year, and then in the second year add the wildflowers from nursery containers.

For quicker but more costly results, you can plant the entire area using plugs of grass and small wildflower plants. Set the plugs approximately 6 inches on center and plant the wildflowers in groups randomly throughout. For the most natural appearance, grasses should make up about 70 percent of the lawn.

Plantings of native grasses can be maintained at the natural height of the plants, or they can be mown occasionally for a more turflike appearance. For the least mainte-nance, choose a species that grows only to a height that is acceptable to you. Remember that you can always cut a grass shorter on occasion.

Sheep fescue (in the fine fescue group) reaches a height of only about 10 inches, so it can be left unmown. But if you prefer a more even appearance, you can cut it back several times a year. In this wood-land garden, its tolerance of shade is apparent, as it forms a soft carpet under-neath the trees. It needs no fertilizer and is drought tolerant once established.

Buffalo grass is suited to the central part of the United States from Montana and the Dakotas down to New Mexico, Arizona, Texas, and Louisiana. Improved varieties grow only 4 to 6 inches tall. It is fine-textured, is drought tolerant, and does not need to be fertilized, yet it still forms a solid swath of green.

To add interest to a native lawn, place clumps of wildflowers here and there. Mexican hat *(Ratibida columnifera),* which blooms summer to fall, provides color among the blue grama in this Southwest lawn.

A failing lawn in Pasadena, California, was replaced with native Berkeley sedge *(Carex tumulicola).* This clumping, evergreen plant reaches a maximum of 18 inches in height and makes a good ground cover under trees, as it withstands root competition and tolerates sun or shade. This planting has been left to grow and flower, but it can be cut a few times a year to neaten it up.

Another drought-tolerant native is side-oats grama *(Bouteloua curtipendula),* which reaches almost 2 feet in height in late summer, when it sends up seed stems with dancing orange flowers along the sides. It is native to nearly all of the United States except for upper California, the Pacific Northwest, Georgia, and Florida.

MEADOWLIKE LAWNS

The term "meadow" conjures up different images for different people, and in fact, the term is used to describe various natural and cultivated plantings—from expanses of flower-strewn grassland surrounded by alpine peaks to woodland clearings dotted with wildflowers. Likewise, in natural-gardening circles, "meadow" may be used to describe various types of grassy plantings, both native and nonnative.

Simply put, in nature a meadow is an open, sunny area filled with grasses, sedges, and wildflowers that are knee high or a little taller, with shrubs and trees at the margins. The word comes from the Old English *medwe,* which means a piece of land covered with grass and cropped for hay or used as pasture.

The French word for meadow is *prairie.* Although in English the words are used interchangeably, there is a major difference: A prairie is a climax community (the last stage in an evolutionary succession of native plants) that mainly exists in the North American Midwest, and many of the plants are much taller (up to 6 feet) than those found in a typical meadow in the eastern United States. In all but the Great Plains states, to maintain a meadow as a grassland, you must cut or burn once a year to prevent the natural succession of woody species.

In England, before lawns were developed, meadows were cut with scythes to a height of about 4 inches. Beginning in the late 1800s, meadows were gradually replaced with grass-only lawns. The introduction of the gasoline-powered mower in 1902 meant that these grass expanses could be continuously mowed to a uniform height. While meadows contained hundreds of grass and wildflower species, lawns had only two or three different species of grasses.

In North American gardens, what we call meadows are natural-looking areas of grassy planting, with flowering plants providing spots of color among the grasses. They provide a constantly changing display through the seasons and should be cut or burned only once a year, in early spring. Although this style of garden may look too unkempt for some tastes, especially when contrasted with traditional lawns and bedding schemes, a meadow can be a wonderful, lush, and exuberant addition to the garden.

The flowers glow warmly in this Southwest meadow lawn, which was created with a mixture of wildflowers and western wheatgrass *(Agropyron smithii),* a cool-season native. Some of the flowers include African daisy *(Dimorphotheca sinuata),* coreopsis, scarlet flax *(Linum rubrum),* and bachelor's buttons *(Centaurea).*

Here's a nonnative combination that can be used in most parts of the country: daylilies and blue oat grass *(Helictotrichon sempervirens).*

A combination of sedges and ferns creates a walkable lawn in a shady San Francisco backyard. Silver variegated Japanese sedge *(Carex oshimensis* 'Evergold') with Catlin sedge *(C. texensis)* are planted together for variations on a theme. The fern adds a touch of bright green tinged with pink amid the evergreen sedges.

Beautifully suited to the natural stone facing of this house, side-oats grama *(Bouteloua curtipendula)* is one of the few native grasses that is easy to start from seed. In this native garden near Chicago, Illinois, it is used for the "lawn" area; the rest is filled with prairie plants.

In a mixed planting that forms a transition between a sedge lawn and an understory in Vancouver, British Columbia, a single golden wood millet *(Milium effusum* 'Aureum') lights up the shady area beneath the trees.

Annual begonias and coleus are surprising brighteners for a lawn edged with dwarf Japanese sweet flag *(Acorus gramineus* 'Pusillus').

KNEE-HIGHS

Achnatherum hymenoides
INDIAN RICE GRASS (12 TO 14 in.)

A. speciosum
DESERT NEEDLE GRASS (24 in.)

Andropogon virginicus
BROOM SEDGE (12 in.)

Aristida spiciformis
BOTTLEBRUSH THREE-AWN (10 TO 15 in.)

A. stricta
PINELAND THREE-AWN (15 in.)

Bouteloua curtipendula
SIDE-OATS GRAMA (12 TO 24 in.)

Elymus glaucus
BLUE WILD RYE (12 TO 36 in.)

Eragrostis campestris
ELLIOT'S LOVE GRASS (18 TO 24 in.)

E. spectabilis
PURPLE LOVE GRASS (12 TO 18 in.)

Festuca californica
CALIFORNIA FESCUE (18 TO 24 in.)

Koeleria macrantha
HAIR GRASS (16 TO 20 in.)

Muhlenbergia capillaris
PINK MUHLY (12 in.)

M. wrightii
SPIKE MUHLY (18 in.)

Nassella cernua
NODDING NEEDLE GRASS (12 TO 20 in.)

N. lepida
FOOTHILL NEEDLE GRASS (12 TO 20 in.)

N. pulchra
PURPLE NEEDLE GRASS (12 TO 20 in.)

Sporobolus junceus
PINEWOODS DROPSEED (18 in.)

Old manhole covers make unusual stepping-stones across a "pond" of creeping red fescue in this El Cerrito, California, garden. The surrounding "chaparral" landscape is planted with lavender, Santa Cruz Island buckwheat *(Eriogonum arborescens)*, sunflowers, tufted hair grass *(Deschampsia beringensis)*, and *Verbena bonariensis.* Design: Jana Olson Drobinsky.

A mown path through a large meadow is not only pleasant to look at but also provides an easy way to enjoy walking amid the grasses and wildflowers.

In the "Plains Garden" at the Denver Botanic Garden, a mix of grasses dominated by little bluestem *(Schizachyrium scoparium)* turns reddish in fall.

Reaching only 8 to 10 inches in height, blue grama *(Bouteloua gracilis)* is a great choice for a meadowlike lawn. Although native to the Southwest, it can be used in most parts of the country. Here it is combined with red and yellow blanket flower *(Gaillardia × grandiflora* 'Goblin') and paperflower *(Psilostrophe tagetina)*, both of which have a long season of bloom.

Autumn moor grass *(Sesleria autumnalis)* is native to Europe but well adapted to many parts of North America. It can withstand cold winters as far north as Nebraska and tolerates a variety of soils and conditions. It has lime green foliage and blooms from mid-summer to fall with spiky panicles. As seen here, it's an excellent choice for planting in large masses in sun or light shade.

This tall meadowlike lawn includes miscanthus, blue oat grass, and pink muhly *(Muhlenbergia capillaris)*. The muhly grass forms mounds of dark green foliage about 2 feet tall and sends up stunning airy dark pink blooms in fall. The low plants in the foreground include snow-in-summer *(Cerastium tomentosum)*. Designed by Chris Rosmini.

SOME WILDFLOWERS FOR BLENDING

Northeast
BLUE-EYED GRASS *Sisyrinchium bellum*
PRAIRIE SMOKE *Geum triflorum*
PUSSY TOES *Antennaria*

Southeast
BLANKET FLOWER *Gaillardia aristata*
BUTTERFLY WEED *Asclepias tuberosa*
LANCE-LEAFED COREOPSIS *Coreopsis lanceolata*
MEXICAN EVENING PRIMROSE *Oenothera speciosa*

Southwest
DESERT MARIGOLD *Baileya multiradiata*
DESERT ZINNIA *Zinnia grandiflora*
PERKY SUE *Tetraneuris argentea*
PRAIRIE PENSTEMON *Penstemon ambiguus*
SAND VERBENA *Abronia fragrans*

West Coast
BLUE-EYED GRASS *Sisyrinchium bellum*
CALIFORNIA POPPIES *Eschscholzia californica*
NATIVE IRIS *Iris munzii, I. fernaldii, I. purdyi*
TIDYTIPS *Layia platyglossa*

MINIATURE MEADOW MAKEOVER

The owner of this compact San Francisco backyard wanted to have an area in her garden, however small, that could serve several purposes. Because her main view of the

yard came from the deck above, she wanted a cool green foil for her more brightly colored plantings. And she also wanted a place for the neighbor's young children to play. However, the site presented several challenges. The existing turf grass was continually attacked by raccoons digging for grubs. Steep walls rise up on either side, sheltering it, but even when the sun is directly overhead, no more than three-quarters of the space receives direct sun. To maximize the growing space, the previous owners had built several terraces, each of which measured only 4½ by 15 feet. Both the terraces and the surrounding walls are poured concrete, which reflects heat and tends to dry out the soil. Over time, the soil had become compacted and infested with weeds.

"I was amazed at how quickly the grasses filled in."

1   The existing turf grass was killed by several applications of glyphosate, a systemic herbicide that breaks down quickly into the soil. (April)

2   The area was amended with organic compost, which was tilled in to a depth of 4 to 6 inches. Any grubs that turned up were destroyed by hand, to make the area less appealing to the raccoons. (May)

3   The main planting was to be California meadow sedge and Berkeley sedge, both planted from inexpensive plugs. Accent plants and larger grasses were planted from 4-inch and 1-gallon nursery pots. (May)

THE PLANTS

Grasses and grasslike plants
Carex oshimensis 'Evergold'
C. pansa CALIFORNIA MEADOW SEDGE
C. tumulicola BERKELEY SEDGE
Briza media COMMON QUAKING GRASS
Festuca muelleri
Hakonechloa macra 'Aureola' JAPANESE
 FOREST GRASS
Panicum virgatum 'Dallas Blues' SWITCH GRASS
Pennisetum alopecuroides 'Moudry'
 BLACK-FLOWERING FOUNTAIN GRASS
Phormium 'Sundowner' NEW ZEALAND FLAX
Sesleria caerulea BLUE MOOR GRASS

Spillers
Cuphea hyssopifolia FALSE HEATHER
Helichrysum petiolare LICORICE PLANT
Lobelia erinus

Blenders
Chamaemelum nobile CHAMOMILE
Galium odoratum SWEET WOODRUFF
Thymophylla tenuiloba DAHLBERG DAISY
Thymus × citriodorus LEMON THYME

4 Fully planted, the plugs were spaced between 6 and 8 inches on center. The entire area was covered with a fine bark mulch and watered two times per week to encourage growth. (May)

5 Within two months, the sedges have completely filled in and the larger grasses have grown dramatically. The raccoons have stayed away. The planting can be mowed or lightly sheared twice a year if needed. If the sedge clumps grow too large, they can easily be dug up and divided. (August)

STAN

...DING TALL

If you are familiar at all with ornamental grasses, it may be because of their widespread use in perennial borders and as wavelike mass plantings. But in addition to these uses, taller grasses and grasslike plants—from knee-high to towering— can also serve as mainstays of an evergreen palette, as ingenious screens and barriers, or as dramatic accents in both small and large spaces. As always, proper plant selection is essential to the art of garden design. There are several things you should know about any grass before using it in your garden.

First among them is probably size. Don't forget that some size listings refer only to the height of the foliage clump; long-lasting flowers may tower several feet above the foliage. Then you must consider the season of bloom, and whether the plant is evergreen or deciduous. Because of its strong structure, even a deciduous grass can continue to provide interest into the winter months (see page 96). Think also of hardiness and suitability for your climate. If there's a tender plant you simply must have in your northern garden, treat it as an annual. Finally, there are a host of aesthetic considerations, among them color, texture, flower shape, and overall structure. The images in this chapter show the myriad ways other gardeners have used tall grasses in their garden designs. You're bound to pick up ideas and inspirations for your own.

The various colors and variegations of *Phormium* 'Cream Delight', 'Jester', 'Yellow Wave', and 'Marcia's Purple' along with silver-leafed *Astelia nervosa chathamica* rain down in a hail of foliage. Along the border of the fescue lawn are Japanese sweet flag (*Acorus gramineus* 'Ogon') and *Carex albula*.

DESIGNING WITH GRASSES

The terminology used by garden designers can seem daunting, but chances are that most principles of design are really quite familiar to you. Keep these guidelines in mind when trying to find the right spots in your garden for individual plants, creating pleasing combinations, or designing borders that will hold interest through the year. Most important, experiment with different groupings and situations until you find the style in your garden that pleases you the most.

Informal abundance characterizes this lush garden, filled to the brim with dramatic and colorful plants. Observe how the texture of the flame-colored *Phormium* 'Jester' on the left contrasts with the gray-leafed *Solanum* on the right.

Simplicity is an effective garden principle, but a simple planting doesn't have to be boring. Behind these cobalt chairs is a hedge of golden honeysuckle underplanted with *Hakonechloa macra* 'Aureola'. The colors form a striking but complementary contrast. Design: Virginia Israelit/Michael Schultz.

Observe from different vantage points to see where you might use repetition and create focal points in your plantings. This technique brings order and harmony to the garden.

The grasses and perennials in this planting are of similar hues, which links them as a composition. It is the variation in height, scale, and repetition that draws the eye from one part of the scene to another.

DESIGNER TALK

SCALE The relative size of plants and objects in the garden. Good use of scale can help you achieve balance in your designs.

STRUCTURE Designers often refer to the "bones" of the garden—the basic layout and hardscape that define the garden's shape and major features.

FOCAL POINT Try to create both focal points and destinations in the garden, places to which the eye and the body are drawn.

TEXTURE A plant's texture is based on the heaviness or lightness of its foliage and flowers, from airy to substantial.

SHAPE AND FORM More than just the height and width of a plant, its overall silhouette should influence your planting decisions.

VARIEGATION Because so many grasses are used as foliage plants, look for those with cream, white, yellow, or other stripes and patterns on the leaves.

Allowing your plants to intermingle freely, rather than following rigid lines, can lead to unexpected and delightful "moments" in the garden. Consider both color and texture when placing plants near one another.

It's not only what's inside the garden that matters; so-called borrowed scenery can become integral to your designs. The casual mix of stone, *Alchemilla mollis,* and sedges that lead to this seating area is an echo of the hills beyond.

Designing with Grasses **41**

LIGHT AND MOVEMENT

The flower and seed heads they sport give grasses characteristics not shared by many other garden ornamentals. First, they are remarkably lightweight, swaying and dipping with the wind. Second, they have an ability to catch the light in ways that other plants cannot. Consider the angle and timing of the light when positioning your grasses in the garden. Do you like to sit outdoors at sunset? Then why not plant a bank of waving miscanthus just above the horizon view? Or perhaps you are a morning person, who enjoys a variety of backlit grassy flowers dotted around the breakfast patio.

Look beyond the color of grass flowers to their shapes and textures. The drooping fingerlike flower heads of the miscanthus in this garden could not be more different from the bunny tails of its grassy companion.

Grasses such as this brome grass are grown as humble forage for cattle. As ornamentals, they have seed heads that float and bounce in the breeze, evocative of wider pastures beyond the garden.

Planting masses and sweeps of a single plant is a dramatic and effective way to capture special moments of light. Here, the pink flower panicles of pink muhly *(Muhlenbergia capillaris* 'Regal Mist') become a fiery cloud at sunset.

Beard grass *(Andropogon)* has silky flower heads that shimmer in the light of daybreak. Many grasses with small, delicate-looking flower heads are at their best when caught by the bright light of early morning, the time of day when showier flowers seem washed out by the sun's glare.

The flattened panicles of sea oats *(Uniola paniculata)* delightfully nod and bow on flexible stems.

COLOR ME CRIMSON

Among the multiple colors of grasses are those ranging from pink to almost black.

Flowers

Carex baccans CRIMSON-SEEDED SEDGE
Muhlenbergia capillaris PINK MUHLY
Pennisetum alopecuroides 'Moudry'
Rhynchelytrum repens RUBY GRASS

Foliage

Imperata cylindrica 'Rubra' JAPANESE BLOOD
  GRASS
Miscanthus sinensis 'Purpurascens'
  FLAME GRASS
Pennisetum 'Burgundy Giant'
P. setaceum 'Rubrum'
Phyllostachys nigra BLACK BAMBOO
Phormium (many)
Saccharum SUGARCANE (many)
Uncinia rubra RED HOOK SEDGE

Fall Foliage

Hakonechloa macra 'Aureola' JAPANESE FOREST
  GRASS (above)
Panicum virgatum 'Haense Herms' and
  'Shenandoah' RED SWITCH GRASS
Vetiveria zizanioides VETIVER

Full-feathered flowers—such as those of pampas grass *(Cortaderia),* reed grass *(Calamagrostis),* and some of the large-flowered *Miscanthus*—make a strong statement in the garden.

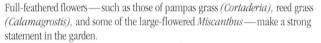

WINNING COMBINATIONS

Of all companion plants, flowering perennials seem naturally to blend well with tall grasses. Those with similar lanky stems and small flower heads, such as lavender, Russian sage, or gaura, make ideal companions in sun-drenched western gardens. Those plants that form mounds of long-lasting blooms, such as penstemon, coneflowers, or rudbeckia, are ideal for mass plantings of five or more of each plant. And flowers with strong punctuations of color, such as dahlias, daylilies, and even phlox and salvias, show up beautifully against a foil of grassy foliage. Among the most important dictates of companion planting is to group species with similar cultural needs close together.

This frothy knee-high mix is fronted by foxtail barley *(Hordeum jubatum),* with buttonlike annual flowers visible through the showy infloresence of the grass.

To make your garden designs interesting without looking cluttered, choose plants of similar habit or flower shape. Below are some characteristics to look for beyond color and size.

| Spires | Daisylike | Frothy | Dramatic | Mounding | Trailing |

Daisylike flowers are among the most plentiful in the horticultural world, with endless variation on the theme. Here, purple coneflower *(Echinacea purpurea)* and blue oat grass *(Helictotrichon sempervirens)* share a sunny spot.

Both *Miscanthus sinensis* 'Variegatus' and Queen of the Prairie *(Filipendula rubra)* require plenty of moisture and rich soil to reach their full heights, which can exceed 6 feet.

When pink muhly flowers into a cloud of pinkish red, it seems to float around the bases of taller plants—in this garden, they include *Dipsacus* and yellow-spired ligularia.

Two very different plants can make a composition. Horsetail *(Equisetum hyemale)* forms a background of deep green for the orange flowers of a dark-leafed dahlia.

The contrast in texture between the threadlike foliage of *Muhlenbergia capillaris* and the stout succulent leaves of *Agave parryi* is what makes this an arresting combination.

GRASSES WITH SHRUBS

Many grasses and grasslike plants can function in the place of shrubs or perennials in the garden. As shrublike plants, they provide structure, permanence, and evergreen color or winter interest. Or they can serve as more changeable perennials amid a mixed border of woody deciduous or evergreen shrubs. One unique aspect of grasses is their airy texture, which allows you to place them in front of or amid denser shrubs without fear that they'll obscure their more substantial partners.

Large variegated grasses are right at home in a border of mixed shrubs. Their mounding shape is similar to that of the surrounding plants, and their luminous foliage and weaving flower stalks add an extra dimension to the border.

The beauty of an informal garden is that you can let plants happily grow between and around each other. Here, blue lyme grass *(Leymus arenarius)* has been infiltrated by a rose—but the grass is sturdy enough not to become overrun.

Roses and grasses make natural companions. Most are sun lovers, and the rose blossoms are enhanced by a grassy background. Here, 'Two Timer' rose is paired with *Miscanthus sinensis* 'Variegatus'.

Shrubs and small trees with dark foliage look spectacular contrasted with the drooping, graceful foliage of the larger grasses. This grass is combined with smoke tree *(Cotinus)*.

Place a grass with a wispy fan of flowers in front of a dramatic plant such as *Rosa* 'Dortmund'. The result is a wonderful new perspective of both plants.

Grasses with Shrubs

A YEARLY EVENT

Annuals in the grassy garden can be thought of in two ways. Although there are very few ornamental annual grasses, a few key choices can be used very well as fillers or midseason replacements in garden borders or containers. On the other hand, many annual flowers and flowering bulbs look particularly striking when paired with midsize grasses in the garden. Think of mingling carex and snowdrops in a shady spring border, for instance, or planting drought-tolerant Mediterranean summer bulbs amid a collection of succulents and grasses.

Self-sowing annuals such as sweet alyssum and *Cerinthe major* send up new plants of their own accord, dappling this sedge lawn with color.

Mondo grass *(Ophiopogon japonicus* and *O. j.* 'Kyoto Dwarf') spills down both sides of a stone staircase. The South African native *Freesia alba,* a sweet-scented bulb, has naturalized in the grasslike lawn, sending up new cup-shaped blossoms each spring.

The bedding schemes of old can be given a modern twist by placing a grassy divide between familiar annuals such as salvia and cockscomb *(Celosia).*

Annuals are known for their bright colors, and here's a combination to heat up the garden—burgundy *Pennisetum setaceum* 'Rubrum', orange-flowered zinnia *(Zinnia angustifolia),* and silver dusty miller.

This meadowlike garden is filled with one of the few annual grasses, *Briza maxima.* Its grassy seed heads quake in the breeze.

Ornamental corn makes a striking and unusual specimen in the annual garden. Varieties of *Zea mays* sport fanciful coloration on both their foliage and the ears they produce at summer's end.

Well-established mixed borders of annuals, perennials, and shrubs line this grassy path. The tender New Zealand flax *(Phormium tenax* 'Yellow Wave') is planted in a pot and overwintered indoors. Behind it rises a plume poppy *(Macleaya cordata)* in full bloom, fronted by miscanthus not yet in flower.

Grassy borders

A well-designed perennial border is considered by many to be the ultimate test of the gardener's skill.

A coherent design, continuous bloom, and the correct selection and placement of plants are all part of successful border planting. Although grasses allow tremendous design flexibility to plant in masses and groups, the fact is that many gardeners want to create traditional beds and borders in their gardens. But what are the rules for borders? And how do grasses fit in?

First, most gardeners prefer either a formal or an informal planting style. The overall effect of an informal planting will be one of abundance and exuberance, which is particularly suitable for naturalistic, cottage-style, and native gardens. At the extreme end of informal are wild plantings, which rely not on structure or shape but rather on a riotous mix of colors and textures.

A formal border, on the other hand, may appear to be better behaved than an informal one, but in fact formal plantings almost always require more input on the part of the gardener to keep them in bounds. Repeated specimens, symmetrical features, and a fairly strict progression of plants from lowest to tallest characterize this style. You may choose to mix formal and less formal elements in these borders, relying on a few key structural elements (either evergreen plants or hardscape) and then mixing in less rigid plantings to soften the effect.

One approach to building a border is to choose plants based on color schemes. The joy of using grasses is that they can often provide the "buffer" colors within a border. Gray or blue, for instance, is often used to temper extreme color contrasts such as pink and yellow, and the soft tan and beige tones of many grass heads also provide a neutral foil for warmer colors such as red, orange, or yellow.

A stone-paved pathway leads to a gate in this Portland, Oregon, garden. What gives the passage a sense of mystery are the tall plants on either side, which include blue oat grass *(Helictotrichon sempervirens)*, at left, and *Miscanthus sinensis* 'Morning Light'. Yellow rudbeckias provide cheerful spots of color. Design: Tom Vetter.

At the Denver Botanic Garden, a grassy border illustrates just how much color these plants can provide. The vibrant red and bronze shades of fountain grass *(Pennisetum setaceum* 'Rubrum') and *Rhynchelytrum nerviglume* 'Pink Crystals' (center), show up beautifully against the cooler tones of *Calamagrostis × acutiflora* 'Karl Foerster', switch grass *(Panicum virgatum), Miscanthus sinensis,* and *M. s.* 'Little Nicky'.

In Suzanne Porter's garden, a densely packed bed provides a feast for the eyes. The composition includes *Phormium* 'Green Jade', daylilies, agastache, 'Siskiyou' blue fescue (front, left), *Miscanthus sinensis* 'Nippon', and feathery *Stipa ramosissima* in the rear.

In Ann Lovejoy's Bainbridge Island, Washington, garden, grasses are woven into a raised bed of shrubs and other flowering plants. This border contains *Miscanthus transmorrisonensis* and lower-growing *Carex flagellifera,* with annuals including nasturtiums and cerinthe in the foreground.

Two grasses with similar colors but very different textures *(Stipa gigantea* and *Nassella tenuifolia)* provide repetition and visual relief amid more brightly colored plants.

Very tall and upright grasses can anchor an entire border composition, as with this tall purple moor grass *(Molinia caerulea arundinacea* 'Skyracer'). Design: Rachel Foster.

Grasses can provide scale and height to create a gradual approach to the ground from towering palms. Pampas grass *(Cortaderia)* can reach 10 feet high; other very tall species include giant reed *(Arundo donax)*, many bamboos, and several *Miscanthus* species.

Part of a border that "steps down" from a tall fence, *Miscanthus sinensis* 'Variegatus' creates a cooling patch of muted green and white amid aster, dahlias, and *Pennisetum alopecuroides* 'Moudry'. Many variegated grasses can be used in this way.

Yellow is a favorite color for gardens in climates with moist air; it seems to glow in subdued light. The lemony variegation of *Cortaderia selloana* 'Sunstripe' is picked up in the spikes of 'Arctic Summer' mullein *(Verbascum bombyciferum)*.

The elements of a successful planting: an ivy-covered wall, a mix of taller grasses in and out of bloom, flowering perennials, and a single urn in the foreground.

A border with a naturalistic flair, this one skillfully mixes and matches with a riotous blend of grasses, succulents, and perennials. On the right is *Chondropetalum tectorum*, to the rear is *Phormium* 'Sea Jade'. *Agave bracteata* and *Echeveria* 'Afterglow' are raised up in a pot, surrounded by lower-growing sea holly *(Eryngium variegata)*, wheatgrass *(Agropyron)*, and Japanese sweet flag *(Acorus gramineus* 'Ogon'). Design: Planet Horticulture.

Carex elata 'Aurea' is perfectly matched with char-treuse aralia, ferns, and burgundy coral bells and loropetalum.

Keeping the palette in a cool mix of greens and yellows, the fine-leafed grasses in front lead to a New Zealand flax behind.

This understory planting by Oehme and Van Sweden Associates contains few plants, but it seems to have a sense of movement that draws the eye toward the trees and the deck. Rising up from a bed of Japanese forest grass *(Hakonechloa macra* 'Aureola') are the flowers of *Hosta* 'Tall Boy'.

In early spring, the still-dormant grasses in this garden are self-effacing partners to displays of spring bulbs, including daffodils and tulips.

As the grasses mature, they add greater volume. Here, maiden grass *(Miscanthus sinensis* 'Gracillimus') and three striped zebra grasses *(M. s.* 'Zebrinus') form a backdrop to gardener's garters *(Phalaris arundinacea* 'Picta').

FOUR-SEASON PLANTINGS

In cold-winter climates, the gardener's rewards are most often realized in spring and summer, when most plants are in active growth. But one of the virtues of ornamental grasses is that as cool weather brings the waning of the more spectacular flower show in the garden, it is the time when many grasses come into their own. That's one reason why grasses and bamboos make such great elements of year-round plantings.

SPRING ARRIVALS

Cool-season grasses, such as the *Calamagrostis, Hakonechloa, Helictotrichon, Melica,* and *Stipa* species, flower earlier than their more temperate relatives. In general, they prefer temperatures that range from 60 to 75°F. They often have a period of bloom in late winter, then spend the hot summer months in dormancy. Many of these early bloomers make subtle contrasts for the showier flowers of spring and early summer. And even those that slow in growth during summer may keep their flowers throughout the hottest months, much like the warm-season growers in winter. Once the temperatures and hours of daylight decrease in fall, you may get another burst of growth from these plants, only to see them retire again when winter truly sets in.

Where winter temperatures are not too severe, cool-season grasses may be evergreen, continuing their growth through the rainy winter season. In a mild climate, it's worth seeking out those grasses that will hold their foliage color throughout the winter, especially low-growing grasses for natural lawns (see pages 28–37).

STRONG IN SUMMER

Warm-season grasses don't begin growth until late spring. This group includes many of the most popular garden types, including *Miscanthus, Molinia, Panicum,* and *Pennisetum* species. When temperatures rise above 80°F, they undergo their greatest period of growth, sometimes doubling or tripling in size in a single sum-

Fall brings plume flowers and a gradual fading from summer's vibrant colors and exuberant growth.

Like tireless sentinels, the grasses stand upright from the snow-covered ground. Their winter hues bring warmth, structure, and interest to this snowy landscape.

because when the bulbs go dormant, the grasses take over; their growth is rapid and vigorous. By midsummer, they are voluptuous and they disguise the fading foliage of many early-blooming perennials. A host of these grasses bloom late in the season, often into October in the warmest climates. Then, with the first few frosts, the foliage fades to shades of tan and almond. Many then hold their form and flowers throughout the winter months.

PLANNED PLANTINGS

Planning a year-round garden takes skill and experience. With forethought, you can create a garden that is not only interesting throughout the seasons, but that seems in harmony with them. In spring, the cool blues, yellows, and peaches of spring show up beautifully against the greenest foliage plants. Summer, especially in the western states, calls for grasses with enough color to stand up to strong direct sunlight, which can make many flowering plants look washed-out and faded. In fall, with the leaves of trees turning brilliant shades, the flowers of most grasses are more subtle variations on a theme. Keep the grasses' growth habits in mind when you plant, too. The best seasons for planting grasses

in mild climates are in early spring, or in fall, when winter rains help develop the root systems that will nourish the plant when it begins growth in spring or summer. In cold-winter climates, it's best to plant in spring after the last hard frost (you can get this date from your local Cooperative Extension Office).

As you experiment with different species and cultivars, you may experience a few losses along the way—grasses felled by extreme summer heat or frozen beyond the point of no return in winter. Fortunately grasses are among the most forgiving of plants—many that look dead seem to rise again when their preferred season of growth resumes. If you are unsure whether a grass has truly died or just gone dormant, cut it back and give it a few months with regular (but not excessive) water. Eventually you'll see evidence of green growth. Grasses that are marginal or tender in your area don't need to be struck off your planting list. Consider digging them up, or putting them in containers that can be brought into a frost-free garage or greenhouse in the winter. Or treat them as annuals, replacing them each spring. Grasses often grown this way include the tender *Pennisetum* species, *Cyperus*, and phormiums.

SPECIMENS AND ACCENTS

Because of their height, particularly when they are flowering, many grasses and grasslike plants are ideal for use as single focal points in the garden. The large miscanthus, pampas grass, and clumping bamboos are commonly planted in this way, serving as punctuation marks beside a pond or a path, or as devices to draw the eye in the distance. Perhaps the most familiar grasslike accent plants are phormiums, which, with their dramatic stiff leaves and striking variegations, are eye-catching in any situation.

Big bluestem *(Andropogon gerardii)* is a prairie grass that can look quite stately as a single specimen in the garden. In this naturalistic setting, surrounded by meadow grasses and flowers, the grass has a subtle yet striking presence.

In fall, big bluestem assumes a different dimension, coming to the fore when its foliage turns a rich coppery color.

It is in winter when the strong structure of many grasses is most evident. A coating of snow makes this pampas grass *(Cortaderia selloana)* glisten in the light.

New Zealand flax is one of the most dramatic and dynamic subjects for accents. The setting at left is tropical and full of hot color; on the right, a citron-colored flax stands stiffly amid a bed of succulents and other grasses. Over time, many of these plants will assume towering dimensions—up to 10 feet or more. Established plants send up branched clusters of tubular flowers that rise up to twice the height of the foliage—providing even more drama.

Notable both for its overall size and its magnificent flower plumes, cold-hardy ravenna grass *(Saccharum ravennae)* stands tall at pondside.

Bamboos make their presence known with their long, arching stems, upright shape, and copious foliage. A single plant placed in a pot can make a garden seem lush and plentiful, as well as lending an Asian air to the scene (see page 91).

Screens

A good screen must have several characteristics. It must be dense, tall, and fast growing. In most cases, it is best if the screen is evergreen, to provide year-round visual protection from nearby utilities, sheds, or other dwellings. Many grasses fit this description and offer an added bonus: Their rustling foliage can also provide a pleasant low level of sound to drown out objectionable noises, such as passing traffic.

An effective screen doesn't need to be evergreen to obscure or soften an unsightly feature year-round. This dormant miscanthus turns a plain wall into a focal point even in winter.

Black bamboo *(Phyllostachys nigra* 'Hinon') towers behind this border planting in Eugene, Oregon, completely concealing what lies behind.

Miscanthus sinensis 'Strictus' is an effective hedge behind this seating area. With a tall, upright habit, it can grow up to 9 feet.

In John Greenlee's garden in Pomona, California, a sheltered tunnel of bamboo is effectively doubled in length by means of a cleverly placed mirror.

Tall grasses placed beside a path can selectively block portions of the view, creating curiosity as to what lies beyond. In this seaside garden, a row of closely planted reed grass *(Calamagrostis)* creates a small-scale screen.

GRASSES IN MASSES

Thanks to the work of several key designers, many garden lovers have come to recognize the signature sight of grasses planted in grand sweeps (see pages 14–15). This particular design style would seem to have been created expressly for grasses, which boast a uniformity of height and form that few other plants can match. Even if you don't have the space for grand-scale mass plantings, there are effects you can achieve by grouping plants together even in smaller gardens. For a true massed effect, plant odd-numbered specimens in groups, spacing them far enough apart to allow for their quick growth. Or you can overplant, knowing that you can dig up and divide many grasses even after the first year of growth.

This spectacular sweeping vista at Westridge Farms, Langley, British Columbia, contains *Sesleria autumnalis, Carex buchanii,* and blue fescue.

On a clifftop overlooking the Pacific Ocean, a sweeping curve of succulents rises up imposingly from a bed of sweet vernal grass *(Anthoxanthum odoratum)*. Their shape is echoed by the palms in the distance.

Grasses are well suited to country gardens and farms, where they echo the fields and surrounding countryside. The subtle colors of the flower heads harmonize with natural building materials such as stone and wood. This *Deschampsia cespitosa* 'Golden Dew' can be cut back once a year to stimulate new growth.

Stepping down in color, texture, and height, this planting in Pennsylvania contains, clockwise from top: *Arundo donax, Calamagrostis × acutiflora* 'Karl Foerster', *Imperata cylindrica* 'Rubra', *Glyceria maxima* 'Variegata', miscanthus, and *Chasmanthium latifolium*.

Viewed up close, the stiff overlapping leaves of deer grass *(Muhlenbergia rigens)* catch the late-summer light and allow glimpses of *Rudbeckia fulgida* 'Swiss Gold' and feather grass behind. Design: Gary Ratway.

TOUCH
OF STYLE

Somehow grasses seem to find their way into nontraditional garden settings. Perhaps it's their easy cultural needs or their uniformity of appearance. As the gardens on these pages show, there's no reason to limit your tastes to straightforward beds and borders. Add a touch of whimsy, some unique hardscaping, and some objets d'art to create a fun personal outdoor space that reflects your true gardening spirit.

Grasses and bamboos enclose this contemporary canvas pergola. Curving and straight lines intersect, echoing the bending and draping of grassy stems and leaves.

The ebony culms of black bamboo rise out of galvanized pots on a wooden deck. Bamboos with colored stems make effective contemporary accents.

Grass, gravel, and glass are arranged in intersecting lines and panels in this modern geometric patio. The uniformity of low-growing grasses such as sweet flag or grasslike mondo grass makes them suitable for such a conceptual planting.

A simple but striking desert vignette by Carol Shuler contains a curved terra-cotta—colored wall, *Muhlenbergia* 'Regal Mist', and violet silverleaf *(Leucophyllum candidum* 'Thunder Cloud').

A bed of fragrant sweet flag *(Acorus)* is the grassy centerpiece of a 'Mermaid' rose—covered garden hideaway.

In Marcia Donohue's garden, ceramic bamboo mingles with the real thing in a bowling *allée*.

TALL-GRASS MEADOWS

Nothing should be simpler than a return to the way things used to be. Yet when it comes to natural-style gardens, be they prairies or meadows, it can take some time and effort to establish a garden that is self-sustaining. The rewards include the restoration of a native habitat, an increase in wildlife, and a naturalistic appearance in harmony with its surroundings.

By far the best way to establish a meadow planting is to first consult with a local nursery or designer who is familiar with your area. An expert will be able to advise you on site selection, preparation, and—most important— the appropriate plants for your climate and soil. Experts can help you address such issues as zoning regulations (some communities have so-called weed ordinances that seek to prohibit naturalistic plantings), invasiveness, and the amount of upkeep that is required to maintain your meadow garden.

Much of the work of a meadow is involved in the preparation and planting. Weed control is critical; until you become familiar with the plants in your meadow, it can be hard to distinguish them from unwanted weeds. The best defense is to eliminate as many weeds as possible as part of the soil preparation that precedes actual planting.

A grove of trees at the edge of a property can be transformed into a woodland meadow. In this Colorado woodland, quaking *(Populus tremuloides)* float in a sea of grasses, *Calochortus,* and ragwort.

A classic western-style meadow planting includes California poppies and sidalcea.

The traditional tall-grass prairie mix includes Indian grass *(Sorghastrum nutans)* and big bluestem *(Andropogon gerardii)*. Both are clumping, warm-season grasses adapted to a number of different soil types and climate conditions.

In Neil Diboll's Prairie Garden nursery, coneflowers and daisies blend amid the grasses in the setting sun.

MEADOW BASICS

- Choose your site carefully. A meadow garden should be in a sunny, open location.

- Understand the local conditions. The combination of grasses and flowers you choose will depend on your location, your climate, and the soil in your garden.

- Seek local advice. For recommendations on plant selection, preparation, and planting, review the material in these pages, refer to the "Sources" guide on pages 126 to 127, and find a supplier or prairie specialist who is familiar with your area.

- Determine the best planting time for your area. Generally, the best planting times are spring and fall.

- Decide on seeds or plugs. Seeds cost less money to cover a large area, but plugs establish more quickly.

- Prepare the site. Nothing is more important than improving the soil and eradicating as many weeds as possible.

- Take care of the newly established meadow garden. Mulching, weeding, and watering are essential for the first few months after planting.

- If permitted in your area, use fire for occasional renewal of your meadow. Burning or mowing regularly mimics the natural process in a meadow or prairie, and increases the growth and health of your desirable meadow species while discouraging undesirable weeds.

With their adaptability, ease of culture, and sheer visual delight, grasses are handy problem solvers for a variety of garden situations. Whether the challenge is to find a pleasing

FOR EVERY
GARDEN

plant combination to create a certain effect, to find the perfect plant for a particularly challenging spot, or to overcome a deficiency of soil, climate, or site layout, there is a grass that will do the job. In this chapter, you'll find solutions for such tricky questions, along with lists of other plants that blend handsomely with their grassy companions in similar situations.

Grasses are often the perfect choice for a difficult site such as a windswept hillside, a sun-baked coastal garden, or a dry, shady corner. By incorporating these plants into your palette, you can turn a sparse planting into one that looks lush and inviting. And because so many grasses grow quickly, often you can achieve the effect you want in less time than you expect.

Tough and attractive, ornamental grasses are well suited to just about any garden. It's no wonder nurseries throughout the country are stocking up on more of these low-maintenance beauties.

This colorful, texturally rich border demonstrates the many roles grasses can play in the garden. Planted as a screen, golden bamboo *(Phyllostachys aurea)* also serves as a lush backdrop for the mixed planting before it, which features a buff-colored cloud of Mexican feather grass *(Nassella tenuissima)*. Japanese blood grass *(Imperata cylindrica* 'Rubra') provides low vertical accents and harmonizes the red geraniums and purple *Verbena bonariensis.*

BY THE SEA

Coastal living may be easy on people, but it can be tough on plants. Sandy soil dries out quickly and doesn't hold the nutrients that plants need. Constant or intermittently strong winds can break stems and shatter flowerheads. Salt spray can travel inland several miles to damage foliage. And plants may be exposed to unrelenting sun and the reflected heat of light-colored sand.

Grasses in general are tolerant of adverse conditions, and many thrive in coastal settings (see lists on facing page). Their narrow, flexible leaves bend in the wind without breaking and offer less surface area for salt spray to land. But in any coastal planting it's a good idea to improve the moisture retention of sandy soils by adding organic materials such as compost. If possible, shelter plants from the wind by siting them in the lee of structures or larger plants.

A natural choice for seaside gardens in warm areas is New Zealand flax. This resilient plant tolerates winds, drought, and poor soil, growing well even on sunny slopes. A wide range of colors is available, from yellows and greens to dark reds and browns, many variegated with pink and cream tones.

Rugged, dependable daylilies and miscanthus line an oceanside boardwalk. When the breeze picks up, their grassy leaves mimic the motion of waves.

American beach grass, native to the East Coast of North America, adds a touch of green between garden and shoreline. Here it graces a sandy strip on Lake Michigan.

Woven into a bed of colorful perennials, miscanthus stands up to coastal winds and salt spray. Its creamy plumes seem to splash up from a fountain of leaves.

DUNE DUTY

These tough customers can be planted in the sandiest plots, where they'll help to stabilize the soil; larger plants can also help to block the wind. Check with your local Cooperative Extension Office before planting on dunes.

Ammophila breviligulata AMERICAN BEACH GRASS
Armeria maritima COMMON THRIFT
Carex pansa CALIFORNIA MEADOW SEDGE
C. testacea ORANGE NEW ZEALAND SEDGE
Elymus magellanicus MAGELLAN WHEATGRASS
Eragrostis curvula WEEPING LOVE GRASS
Leymus arenarius BLUE LYME GRASS
L. condensatus 'Canyon Prince'
  CANYON PRINCE WILD RYE
L. mollis SEA LYME GRASS
Muhlenbergia capillaris PINK MUHLY
Panicum virgatum SWITCH GRASS
Pennisetum villosum FEATHERTOP
Phalaris arundinacea 'Picta' RIBBON GRASS
Uniola paniculata SEA OATS

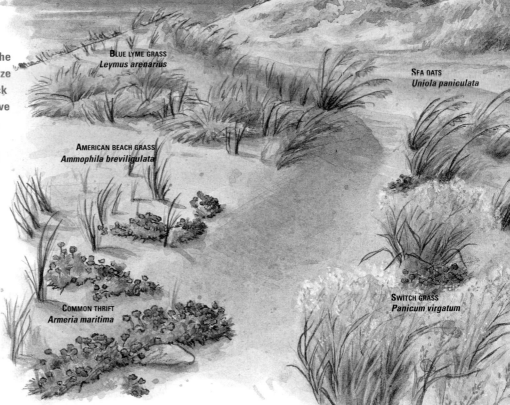

BLUE LYME GRASS
Leymus arenarius

SEA OATS
Uniola paniculata

AMERICAN BEACH GRASS
Ammophila breviligulata

COMMON THRIFT
Armeria maritima

SWITCH GRASS
Panicum virgatum

FOR COASTAL GARDENS

Andropogon ternarius SPLIT-BEARD BROOM SEDGE
Arundo donax GIANT REED
Calamagrostis nutkaensis PACIFIC REED GRASS
Chondropetalum tectorum CAPE RUSH
Cortaderia richardii TUSSOCK GRASS
C. selloana PAMPAS GRASS
Deschampsia cespitosa beringensis
  TUFTED HAIR GRASS
Elegia capensis BROOM REED
Erianthus contortus BENT-AWN PLUME GRASS
Festuca amethystina LARGE BLUE FESCUE
F. californica CALIFORNIA FESCUE
F. glauca COMMON BLUE FESCUE
F. rubra RED FESCUE
F. valesiaca 'Glaucantha' WALLIS FESCUE
Helictotrichon sempervirens BLUE OAT GRASS
Hemerocallis DAYLILY
Kniphofia RED-HOT POKER
Liriope and *Ophiopogon*
Miscanthus 'Giganteus' GIANT SILVER GRASS
M. sinensis
Molinia caerulea MOOR GRASS
Muhlenbergia dumosa BAMBOO MUHLY
M. pubescens SOFT BLUE MEXICAN MUHLY
M. rigens DEER GRASS

Nassella lepida FOOTHILL NEEDLE GRASS
N. pulchra PURPLE NEEDLE GRASS
N. tenuissima MEXICAN FEATHER GRASS
Pennisetum alopecuroides FOUNTAIN GRASS
Phormium tenax NEW ZEALAND FLAX
Rhynchelytrum nerviglume NATAL RUBY GRASS
Saccharum ravennae RAVENNA GRASS
Sesleria autumnalis AUTUMN MOOR GRASS
S. caerulea BLUE MOOR GRASS
S. heufleriana BLUE-GREEN MOOR GRASS
Setaria palmifolia PALM GRASS
Spartina pectinata 'Aureomarginata'
  GOLDEN-EDGED PRAIRIE CORD GRASS
Stenotaphrum secundatum 'Variegatum'
  VARIEGATED ST. AUGUSTINE GRASS
Stipa ramosissima PILLAR OF SMOKE
Themeda japonica THEMEDA
Tripsacum dactyloides EASTERN GAMA GRASS
T. floridana FLORIDA GAMA GRASS
Typha angustifolia NARROW-LEAFED CATTAIL
T. minima MINIATURE CATTAIL
Vetiveria zizanioides VETIVER
Yucca filamentosa ADAM'S NEEDLE

COASTAL COMPANIONS

Aloe
Arctostaphylos MANZANITA
Artemisia
Baptisia FALSE INDIGO
Chrysanthemum
Crambe
Echinops GLOBE THISTLE
Erigeron FLEABANE
Eryngium SEA HOLLY
Gaura
Gazania
Hebe
Helianthemum SUNROSE
Juniperus JUNIPER
Lavandula LAVENDER
Limonium STATICE
Lupinus LUPINE
Myosotidium
Myrica
Narcissus
Osteospermum AFRICAN DAISY
Phlomis
Rosa rugosa
Santolina
Sedum STONECROP
Solidago GOLDENROD
Stachys

Hot and dry

Grasses once covered the huge midsection of North America, thriving in hot and dry conditions for countless years. Some of these noble survivors— like Indian grass, little bluestem, and big bluestem—make great garden choices for sunny spots that get little irrigation. Good drainage is a must for these plants, so amend the soil with plenty of organic matter before planting. Some grasses that thrive in heat also need a period of winter chill to give their best performance (see page 9).

Dry-themed gardens can be created by combining drought-tolerant grasses with appropriate partners such as cypress and lavender for a Mediterranean look, or cacti, succulents, and some open ground to evoke the desert. A gravel mulch helps improve drainage, and a smattering of boulders enhances the dry theme.

Designed to replace a conventional lawn, this planting is unfazed by high temperatures and low rainfall. A central patch of blue grama is bounded on the right by the beige flowers of common blue fescue. Atop the gentle slope, Indian grass and lavender make a pretty pair.

Deer grass, a Western native, looks right at home among cacti and penstemon. An occasional soaking will help it reach its full size of 4 feet high and wide, but established plants will survive and grow without irrigation.

A flagstone path winds through a mixed planting of grasses and perennials that flourish in hot and dry conditions. Many heat-loving plants have light blue or gray leaves, which reflect the sun's heat while adding cool tones to the garden palette.

This member of the *Agave* family, red yucca, pairs a grassy effect with colorful blooms. A tough plant that thrives in even the hottest situations, it needs only an occasional deep soaking and removal of spent flowers to look handsome year round.

FOR HOT, DRY GARDENS

Achnatherum speciosum INDIAN RICE GRASS
Andropogon gerardii BIG BLUESTEM
A. saccharoides SILVER BEARD GRASS
A. ternarius SPLIT-BEARD BROOM SEDGE
Bouteloua gracilis BLUE GRAMA
Buchloe dactyloides BUFFALO GRASS
Chloris virgata FINGER GRASS
Cortaderia selloana 'Pumila' COMPACT PAMPAS GRASS
Dasylirion quadrangulatum MEXICAN GRASS TREE
D. wheeleri DESERT SPOON
Festuca glauca COMMON BLUE FESCUE
F. muelleri MUELLER'S FESCUE
Hesperaloe parviflora RED YUCCA
Leymus arenarius BLUE LYME GRASS
Muhlenbergia lindheimeri LINDHEIMER'S MUHLY
M. rigens DEER GRASS
Nassella cernua NODDING NEEDLE GRASS
N. lepida FOOTHILL NEEDLE GRASS
N. pulchra PURPLE NEEDLE GRASS
N. tenuissima MEXICAN FEATHER GRASS
Pennisetum setaceum TENDER FOUNTAIN GRASS
Phormium tenax NEW ZEALAND FLAX
Schizachyrium scoparium LITTLE BLUESTEM
Sorghastrum nutans INDIAN GRASS
Sporobolus airoides ALKALI DROPSEED
S. wrightii GIANT SACATON
Stipa capillata FEATHER GRASS
S. gigantea GIANT FEATHER GRASS

* Extremely drought tolerant once established.

HOT AND DRY COMPANIONS

Achillea YARROW
Agave
Aloe
Arctostaphylos MANZANITA
Artemisia
Banksia
Coreopsis
Euphorbia
Fallugia APACHE PLUME
Gaura
Helianthemum SUNROSE
Lavandula LAVENDER
Leucospermum PINCUSHION
Marrubium
Oenothera EVENING PRIMROSE
Opuntia
Penstemon
Perovskia RUSSIAN SAGE
Phlomis
Protea
Rosmarinus ROSEMARY
Santolina
Sedum STONECROP
Thymus THYME

GIANT SACATON
Sporobolus wrightii

ALKALI DROPSEED
Sporobolus airoides

DEER GRASS
Muhlenbergia rigens

PINELEAF PENSTEMON
Penstemon pinifolius

Santolina rosmarinifolia

Santolina rosmarinifolia

BUFFALO GRASS
Buchloe dactyloides

Agave victoriae-reginae

Made for the shade

Although most grasses prefer a sunny spot, quite a few thrive in partial or dappled shade—and a handful actually require shade to look their best. Particularly well represented among shade-loving grasslike plants are the sedges (Carex) and woodrushes (Luzula). Many bamboos also do best in dappled light.

In a shade garden, where showy flowers are rare, light or variegated foliage provides color and textural contrasts. Elegant, arching blades of grass complement other denizens of moist, shady gardens, such as broadleafed hostas and more delicate ferns. Arrange shade-tolerant flowering grasses among stepping-stones to create a lush woodland walkway beneath trees. Or tuck shade lovers such as sedges or sweet flag (Acorus) into shady pockets in a mixed border of shrubs and perennials. You'll know if your grasses are getting too much shade; they'll grow weakly and flop over (see page 120).

Repeated bursts of grassy leaves provide structure in this shady garden. In the foreground are greater woodrush (right) and variegated sweet flag (left); great drooping sedge towers above the scene.

WILD OATS
Chasmanthium latifolium

BOTTLEBRUSH GRASS
Hystrix patula

HOSTA
SUM AND SUBSTANCE

MOP-HEADED SEDGE
Carex caryophyllea The Beatles

SNOWY WOODRUSH
Luzula nivea

UMBRELLA BAMBOO
Fargesia murielae

LIGHTEN UP!

Try one of these colorful characters for a splash of brightness in a dim corner of the garden. Their gold or silver foliage holds its color throughout the growing season, and their upright form makes a cheerful sight, like a glowing fountain.

A mature clump of striped broad-leafed sedge *(Carex siderosticha* 'Variegata') is an eye-catching accent in the shade.

Japanese forest grass *(Hakonechloa macra* 'Aureola'), one of the most beautiful ornamental grasses, forms a graceful foot-high clump of arching leaves striped green and yellow.

Versatile and colorful, variegated lily turf *(Liriope muscari* 'Variegata') offers violet blooms that stand out well against its yellow-edged leaves.

GOLDEN WOOD MILLET
Milium effusum 'Aureum'

PALM SEDGE
Carex muskingumensis

WILD GINGER
Asarum caudatum

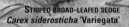
STRIPED BROAD-LEAFED SEDGE
Carex siderosticha 'Variegata'

SWORD FERN
Polystichum munitum

FOR SHADY AREAS

Acorus gramineus JAPANESE SWEET FLAG
Alopecurus pratensis 'Variegatus'
 YELLOW FOXTAIL GRASS
Arrhenatherum elatius bulbosum 'Variegatum'
 STRIPED BULBOUS OAT GRASS
Calamagrostis brachytricha
 FALL-BLOOMING REED GRASS
Carex baccans CRIMSON-SEEDED SEDGE
C. caryophyllea 'The Beatles' MOP-HEADED
 SEDGE
C. comans NEW ZEALAND HAIR SEDGE
C. conica 'Marginata'
 MINIATURE VARIEGATED SEDGE
C. elata 'Aurea' BOWLE'S GOLDEN SEDGE
C. elegantissima 'Variegata'
 GOLDEN-EDGED SEDGE
C. flacca BLUE SEDGE
C. grayi GRAY'S SEDGE
C. morrowii expallida
 VARIEGATED JAPANESE SEDGE
C. muskingumensis PALM SEDGE
C. pansa CALIFORNIA MEADOW SEDGE

C. pendula GREAT DROOPING SEDGE
C. pensylvanica PENNSYLVANIA SEDGE
C. phyllocephala 'Sparkler' SPARKLER SEDGE
C. plantaginea PLANTAIN-LEAFED SEDGE
C. siderosticha 'Variegata' STRIPED
 BROAD-LEAFED SEDGE
C. stricta TUSSOCK SEDGE
C. sylvatica FOREST SEDGE
C. texensis CATLIN SEDGE
C. tumulicola BERKELEY SEDGE
Chasmanthium latifolium WILD OATS
Deschampsia cespitosa TUFTED HAIR GRASS
D. flexuosa CRINKLED HAIR GRASS
Festuca rubra RED FESCUE
Hakonechloa macra JAPANESE FOREST GRASS
Holcus mollis 'Variegatus' CREEPING SOFT GRASS
Hystrix patula BOTTLEBRUSH GRASS
Iris foetidissima GLADWIN IRIS
Liriope LILY TURF
Luzula luzuloides WOODRUSH
L. nivea SNOWY WOODRUSH
L. purpurea PURPLE WOODRUSH

L. sylvatica GREATER WOODRUSH
Milium effusum 'Aureum' GOLDEN WOOD MILLET
Ophiopogon japonicus MONDO GRASS
Poa chaixii FOREST BLUEGRASS
Sesleria autumnalis AUTUMN MOOR GRASS
S. caerulea BLUE MOOR GRASS
S. heufleriana BLUE-GREEN MOOR GRASS
S. nitida GRAY MOOR GRASS
Setaria palmifolia PALM GRASS

SHADE-TOLERANT BAMBOOS

Arundinaria
Chimonobambusa marmorea
Fargesia
Hibanobambusa
Indocalamus
Pleioblastus
Pseudosasa
Sasa
Sasaella
Sasamorpha borealis
Shibataea kumasaca
Thamnocalamus spathiflorus

Wild oats may be the most shade tolerant of all grasses, forming clumps to 2 feet tall and wide. In summer, delightful oat-like flowers rise well above the foliage.

Side yards can be challenging parts of the garden. Often shaded by walls and fences, these areas may fall into neglect. A good solution is to plant shade-tolerant grasses such as those listed above.

Dry shade

All plants need light and water, where both these essentials are reduced, the challenges of gardening can seem daunting. But even in areas of dry shade, such as beneath trees or alongside buildings or concrete patios, it's possible to have a gorgeous garden. The key is to choose plants that are adapted to these austere conditions. To transform a barren corner into a charming nook, try a few of the grassy plants mentioned here.

Greater woodrush *(Luzula sylvatica* 'Marginata') spreads to form a thick carpet in the shade of a tree. Most of the woodrushes do well in dry, shady sites. A few members of the sedge family, such as Pennsylvania sedge and Berkeley sedge, are also good choices for these difficult conditions.

The grassy leaves of Douglas iris (above) and other Pacific Coast irises remain green throughout most of the year. Flowering in spring, these low-growing plants need little if any irrigation and do best in light to dappled shade. Gladwin iris is another excellent candidate for dry shade; it offers flowers in spring and showy seed capsules in fall.

Native to eastern American woodlands, bottlebrush grass is perfectly suited to low levels of light and water, and its delicate flower heads are long-lasting. Other choices from the category of true grasses include crinkled hair grass, creeping soft grass, autumn moor grass, blue-green moor grass, and palm grass.

SMALL WATER FEATURES

Every garden has room for a water feature, but that doesn't mean you have to spend a lot of money or time to create one. Grasses are naturals for use in or near water: Upright, spiky plants rising from a shallow bowl create instant container drama, and those with a drooping habit offer fascinating reflections of leaves or flowers when planted near the water's still surface. A small fountain bubbling among soft grasses soothes the ear as well as the eye. Even a birdbath looks more inviting when surrounded by grassy plants.

Each of these Chinese water bowls has its own function. One is home to a small assortment of aquatic plants, including miniature cattail and a small water iris, and the other reflects the leaves of the bamboo growing beside it.

The sleek lines of this birdbath are enhanced by the stones beneath it and the ornamental grasses behind it. The three elements create an elegant modern composition.

A whimsical water feature peeks out from a mixed border featuring a variegated miscanthus. In the foreground, arching stems of variegated Solomon's seal *(Polygonatum odoratum* 'Variegatum') echo the curve of the miscanthus leaves.

A diminutive statue seems to float before a curtain of miniature cattails in a water-filled glazed bowl.

JUST ADD WATER

These small grassy plants grow well in constantly moist soil or shallow water, making them ideal for growing in bowls or urns.

Acorus gramineus JAPANESE SWEET FLAG
Carex elata 'Aurea' BOWLES' GOLDEN SEDGE
C. muskingumensis PALM SEDGE
C. nigra BLACK-FLOWERING SEDGE
C. nudata CALIFORNIA BLACK-FLOWERING SEDGE
C. pseudocyperus CYPERUS SEDGE
Cyperus albostriatus BROAD-LEAFED
 UMBRELLA PLANT
Eleocharis acicularis SLENDER SPIKE RUSH
Equisetum scirpoides DWARF HORSETAIL
E. hyemale HORSETAIL
Juncus effusus 'Spiralis' CORKSCREW RUSH
J. patens CALIFORNIA GRAY RUSH
Phalaris arundinacea 'Feesey'
 and 'Woods Dwarf' RIBBON GRASS
Scirpus cernuus FIBER OPTICS PLANT
Typha minima MINIATURE CATTAIL

Horsetail *(Equisetum hyemale)* is an extremely invasive plant that spreads rapidly and is almost impossible to eradicate, but the bright green leaves and horizontal banding make it hard to resist. Contain this dangerous beauty in a decorative pot or behind a concrete barrier to bring a touch of the prehistoric into your garden.

It's easy to see why "fiber optics plant" is the common name for *Scirpus cernuus,* a sedge from the British Isles. Tiny flowers held at the tips of threadlike leaves capture the light and seem to glow.

IN AND AROUND WATER

Whether poolside or in the pond, grasses are perfect companions to water. For a naturalistic approach, incorporate grasses in plantings along the pond's edge. Larger ornamental grasses can be used to help soften the boundary between water and land. A number of grassy plants will grow in standing water; these aquatics are best planted in sunken containers. Smaller aquatic plants are discussed on pages 78 to 79.

The soil next to an artificial water feature may actually be quite dry, so it can be tricky to make a natural-looking transition from water-loving to drought-tolerant plantings. A solution is to plant aquatic grasses in the pond, then carry the grassy theme onto land with plants that look similar but have different cultural needs. For ideas on planting the transitional pondside area, see "Sunny Bogs" on page 82.

Surrounding a garden pond is a medley of moisture-loving grasses, including (clockwise from top) stately clumps of miscanthus and black-flowering fountain grass *(Pennisetum alopecuroides* 'Moudry'). Narrow-leafed cattail spreads to fill in the areas nearest the water, and low mounding clumps of black-eyed Susan *(Rudbeckia fulgida)* provide the perfect visual foil for the grasses' tall and upright leaves.

Softening the edges of a formal pool, this planting scheme mirrors the more naturalistic one at left. In the background, miscanthus serves as a screen, flanked by a fountain grass *(Pennisetum alopecuroides* 'Hameln') that is less likely to spread than its counterpart in the wilder garden. In place of cattail — and adding a spiky purple accent — is gayfeather *(Liatris spicata)*. The billowing form of *Coreopsis verticillata* 'Moonbeam' makes is especially pleasing in front of taller grasses.

The remarkable diversity of grasses is evident in this lush planting. In full and glorious flower, a miscanthus takes center stage, while upright *Stipa gigantea*, at left, shows off its towering bloom. The yellow of the low-growing variegated bamboo at left is repeated by the variegated iris at pool's center.

Drought-tolerant bear grass *(Nolina microcarpa)* is paired with *Agave geminiflora* in this striking poolside planting, which reflects a desert theme.

Planted in a sunken container, dwarf papyrus *(Cyperus prolifer)* shows off its golden flowers. A classic aquatic plant, papyrus brings a tropical feel to any pond or pool.

FOR PONDS AND POOLS

Acorus calamus SWEET FLAG
*Carex riparia GREATER POND SEDGE
C. spissa SAN DIEGO SEDGE
C. stricta TUSSOCK SEDGE
*Cyperus alternifolius UMBRELLA PLANT
*C. papyrus PAPYRUS
C. prolifer DWARF PAPYRUS
C. testacea SLENDER PAPYRUS
Eleocharis dulcis CHINESE WATER CHESTNUT
*Glyceria maxima 'Variegata' VARIEGATED
  MANNA GRASS
Iris laevigata
*I. pseudacorus YELLOW FLAG
I. versicolor BLUE FLAG
I. virginica SOUTHERN BLUE FLAG
Juncus effusus SOFT RUSH
J. polyanthemus AUSTRALIAN GRAY RUSH
Schoenoplectus subterminalis SWAYING RUSH
S. tabernaemontani GREAT BULRUSH
*Typha angustifolia NARROW-LEAFED CATTAIL
*T. latifolia COMMON CATTAIL
*T. minima MINIATURE CATTAIL
Zizania aquatica ANNUAL WILD RICE
Z. latifolia ASIAN WILD RICE

AQUATIC COMPANIONS

Aponogeton distachyus WATER HAWTHORN
*Azolla filiculoides FAIRY MOSS
Caltha palustris MARSH MARIGOLD
Colocasia esculenta TARO
Crinum americanum SOUTHERN SWAMP LILY
Marsilea quadrifolia WATER CLOVER
Myriophyllum aquaticum PARROT FEATHER
Nelumbo LOTUS
Nymphaea WATER LILY
*Petasites japonicus JAPANESE COLTSFOOT
*Pistia stratiotes WATER LETTUCE
Pontederia cordata PICKEREL WEED
*Sagittaria ARROWHEAD
Zantedeschia aethiopica COMMON CALLA

*These plants may become invasive, so check with your local Cooperative Extension Office before purchasing or planting.

SUNNY BOGS

Bogs are open spaces where the soil is saturated and the drainage is very poor. Organic residue collects in these spots, creating acidic conditions that few plants can tolerate. A number of grasses and grasslike plants are good choices for these conditions; they soak up the extra moisture like sponges. Some spread vigorously, but their growth is checked where the soil becomes drier. A low spot where soil is often mucky is ideal for planting a bog garden. Or you can transform a leaky artificial pool or pond by filling it with soil and bog plants, and keeping it well watered.

Adding spectacular contrasts in form and color to this boggy garden are variegated irises and Bowles' golden sedge *(Carex elata 'Aurea')*.

FOR SUNNY BOGS

Acorus calamus SWEET FLAG
A. gramineus JAPANESE SWEET FLAG
Andropogon glomeratus BUSHY BEARD GRASS
Arundo donax GIANT REED
Carex baccans CRIMSON-SEEDED SEDGE
C. elata 'Aurea' BOWLES' GOLDEN SEDGE
C. nigra BLACK-FLOWERING SEDGE
C. pendula GREAT DROOPING SEDGE
C. pseudocyperus CYPERUS SEDGE
Chondropetalum tectorum CAPE RUSH
Cortaderia richardii TUSSOCK GRASS
Deschampsia cespitosa TUFTED HAIR GRASS
Eriophorum COTTON GRASS
Holcus mollis 'Variegatus' VARIEGATED
  CREEPING SOFT GRASS
IRIS, JAPANESE AND LOUISIANA
I. laevigata
I. pseudacorus YELLOW FLAG

I. versicolor BLUE FLAG
I. virginica SOUTHERN BLUE FLAG
Juncus RUSH
Molinia caerulea MOOR GRASS
Scirpus
Spartina pectinata PRAIRIE CORD GRASS
Tripsacum dactyloides EASTERN GAMA GRASS
T. floridana FLORIDA GAMA GRASS
Typha CATTAIL

BOG COMPANIONS

Aconitum ACONITE
Asclepias incarnata SWAMP MILKWEED
Caltha palustris MARSH MARIGOLD
Chelone lyonii TURTLEHEAD
Lobelia cardinalis CARDINAL FLOWER
Osmunda regalis ROYAL FERN
Rodgersia
Tradescantia virginiana SPIDERWORT
Zantedeschia aethiopica COMMON CALLA

Cotton grass *(Eriophorum angustifolium)*, a member of the sedge family, is native to bogs in northern regions; it needs cold winters to thrive. Once established, it can spread by creeping rhizomes to cover large areas.

YELLOW FLAG
Iris pseudacorus

FEATHER REED GRASS
Calamagrostis x acutiflora

MARSH MARIGOLD
Caltha palustris

SOFT RUSH
Juncus effusus

VARIEGATED MOOR GRASS
Molinia caerulea 'Vari...

JAPANESE SWEET FLAG
Acorus gramineus 'Ogon'

MOIST MEADOWS

Meadows are a bit drier than bogs, so they can support a wider variety of plants. Grasses are usually the dominant players in a meadow, with small flowering plants scattered among them. However, creating a meadow garden is not just a simple matter of tossing out a few handfuls of seeds. You must prepare the site much as you would for a turf lawn (see pages 36 and 67), and do some research to discover the most appropriate meadow plants for your region. Once a meadow garden is established, however, its casual, naturalistic beauty is well worth the initial effort.

Cornflowers and buttercups consort with various grasses in this colorful meadow. Even a small backyard can be planted as a meadow using a balanced mix of grasses and wildflowers.

FOR MOIST MEADOWS

Achnatherum calamagrostis SILVER SPIKE GRASS
Alopecurus pratensis MEADOW FOXTAIL
Briza media COMMON QUAKING GRASS
Calamagrostis × acutiflora FEATHER REED GRASS
Carex caryophyllea 'The Beatles'
  MOP-HEADED SEDGE
C. flacca BLUE SEDGE
C. grayi GRAY'S SEDGE
C. morrowii JAPANESE SEDGE
C. pansa CALIFORNIA MEADOW SEDGE
C. phyllocephala 'Sparkler' SPARKLER SEDGE
C. tumulicola BERKELEY SEDGE
Cortaderia richardii TUSSOCK GRASS
Deschampsia cespitosa TUFTED HAIR GRASS
D. flexuosa CRINKLED HAIR GRASS
Erianthus giganteus SUGARCANE PLUME GRASS
Festuca amethystina LARGE BLUE FESCUE

Hemerocallis DAYLILY
Iris cristata DWARF CRESTED IRIS
I. douglasiana DOUGLAS IRIS
Miscanthus sinensis
M. transmorrisonensis
  EVERGREEN MISCANTHUS
Molinia caerulea MOOR GRASS
Panicum virgatum SWITCH GRASS
Pennisetum alopecuroides FOUNTAIN GRASS
P. a. 'Caudatum' WHITE-FLOWERING
  FOUNTAIN GRASS
P. setaceum 'Rubrum' PURPLE FOUNTAIN GRASS
Saccharum ravennae RAVENNA GRASS
Sesleria autumnalis AUTUMN MOOR GRASS
S. caerulea BLUE MOOR GRASS
S. heufleriana BLUE-GREEN MOOR GRASS
Sisyrinchium californicum YELLOW-EYED GRASS

MEADOW COMPANIONS

Aquilegia canadensis WILD COLUMBINE
Asclepias tuberosa BUTTERFLY WEED
Aster novae-angliae NEW ENGLAND ASTER
Centaurea cyanus CORNFLOWER
Geranium CRANESBILL
Ipheion uniflorum SPRING STAR FLOWER
Monarda BEE BALM
Osmunda
Phlox maculata THICK-LEAF PHLOX
Ranunculus
Ratibida
Rudbeckia hirta GLORIOSA DAISY
Trollius GLOBEFLOWER

Miscanthus sinensis 'Strictus'

DAYLILY
Hemerocallis 'Happy Returns'

BERKELEY SEDGE
Carex tumulicola

Streams wet and dry

Growing along sloping, rocky banks, streamside plants have adapted by sending their roots into the moist soil but keeping their leaves and stems relatively dry. Most can also tolerate the shade provided by water-loving trees and shrubs. Whether the stream is natural or created, its banks are incomplete without grassy plants. For a unique streamside design, try the flowing forms of silvery and orange sedges, accented by rushes and members of the restio family (plants from the southern hemisphere that appreciate plenty of moisture and excellent drainage).

In the absence of water, a dry creek bed provides a flowing visual effect. Place boulders along the edges of a shallow depression dug to suggest the course of a stream, and use smaller stones to represent water. For an authentic look, plant drought-tolerant grasses and ground covers along the edge.

The long, lax leaves of a bronze form of New Zealand hair sedge mimic flowing water.

Japanese blood grass adds vertical texture and vivid color at the head of a backyard stream.

A dry hillside is transformed by this streamlike arrangement of stones and grassy plants. Repeated clumps of phormium anchor the scene, and a grassy perennial, *Tulbaghia simmleri,* adds a splash of pink. Smaller grasses are planted near large stones and benefit from the moisture trapped beneath them.

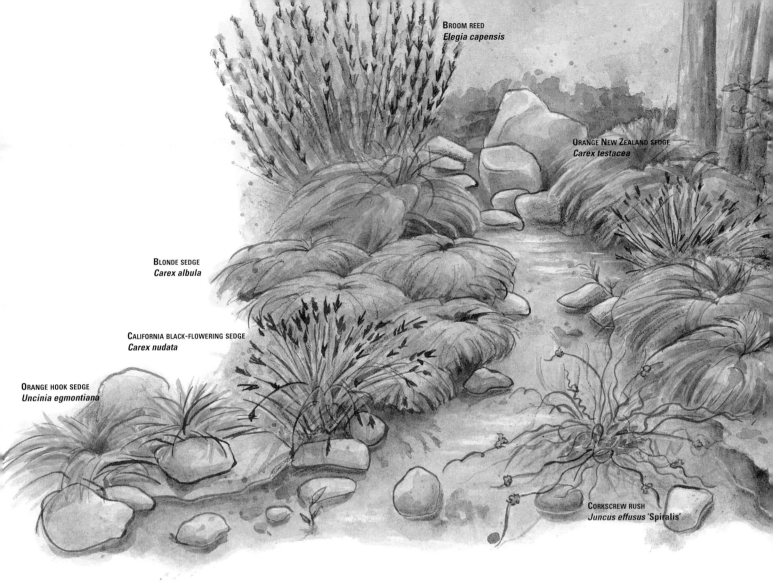

BROOM REED
Elegia capensis

ORANGE NEW ZEALAND SEDGE
Carex testacea

BLONDE SEDGE
Carex albula

CALIFORNIA BLACK-FLOWERING SEDGE
Carex nudata

ORANGE HOOK SEDGE
Uncinia egmontiana

CORKSCREW RUSH
Juncus effusus 'Spiralis'

Members of the rush family, like this California gray rush are naturals for streamside planting. They can grow in standing water but don't mind drying out a bit, so they adapt easily to the changing water levels along a stream's edge.

FOR THE WET STREAMSIDE

*Andropogon glomeratus BUSHY BEARD GRASS
Carex albula BLONDE SEDGE
C. buchananii LEATHER LEAF SEDGE
C. comans NEW ZEALAND HAIR SEDGE
C. flagellifera WEEPING BROWN
  NEW ZEALAND SEDGE
C. muskingumensis PALM SEDGE
C. nudata CALIFORNIA BLACK-FLOWERING SEDGE
C. pendula GREAT DROOPING SEDGE
C. petriei DWARF BROWN NEW ZEALAND SEDGE
*C. testacea ORANGE NEW ZEALAND SEDGE
C. tumulicola BERKELEY SEDGE
Chondropetalum tectorum CAPE RUSH
Deschampsia cespitosa TUFTED HAIR GRASS

Elegia capensis BROOM REED
Festuca mairei ATLAS FESCUE
Hakonechloa macra JAPANESE FOREST GRASS
*Imperata cylindrica 'Rubra' JAPANESE
  BLOOD GRASS
Juncus effusus SOFT RUSH
J. patens CALIFORNIA GRAY RUSH
Miscanthus sinensis EULALIA
*Phalaris arundinacea RIBBON GRASS
Themeda japonica THEMEDA
Uncinia egmontiana ORANGE HOOK SEDGE

*These plants may become invasive, so check with your local Cooperative Extension Office agent before purchasing or planting.

ON SLOPING GROUND

Gardening on an incline presents a special set of challenges. Successful plantings must be fairly drought tolerant, as moisture drains quickly downhill, and they need strong, fast-growing roots to hold the soil against erosion (see facing page). Many grasses meet these challenges and look great doing it.

Hillsides can be planted with sweeps of a single grass, such as Miscanthus transmorrisonensis, which stays green much of the year, or Natal ruby grass (Rhynchelytrum repens), prized for its beautiful pink flowers on drooping stems. Or use a mixed planting scheme, such as purple fountain grass (Pennisetum setaceum 'Rubrum'), which sways in the slightest breeze, set among low-growing, stiff-branched cotoneasters or junipers. New Zealand flax (Phormium tenax), with its bold, stiffly upright leaves in a rainbow of colors, is stunning when paired with gazanias or ground-hugging forms of wild lilac (Ceanothus) or rosemary. Or let a vigorous flowering vine such as honeysuckle spill down the hill, and punctuate the composition with a few upright grasses.

Their graceful flower stalks reaching for the clouds, clumps of blue oat grass *(Helictotrichon sempervirens)* top this hillside planting of blue grama. A rock wall holds the slope and acts as a backdrop for drought-tolerant grasses and penstemons.

Like a sheet of water pouring over a stone wall, aptly named fountain grass *(Pennisetum alopecuroides)* adds grace and a sense of movement to a hillside composition. California fescue *(Festuca californica)* creates a similar flowing effect.

Marching down a gentle slope, sweeps of various grasses in and out of flower serve as accents and blenders in a mixed planting scheme.

HOLDING THE HILLSIDE

Low-growing annual grasses such as ryegrass and brome are often planted for erosion control because they are easy to start from seed and they grow quickly. Like them, the grasses listed below hold the soil with fibrous roots or creeping rhizomes, and their toughness is matched by their beauty.

Andropogon gerardii BIG BLUESTEM
A. ternarius SPLIT-BEARD BROOM SEDGE
A. virginicus BROOM SEDGE
Bouteloua curtipendula SIDE-OATS GRAMA
Buchloe dactyloides BUFFALO GRASS
Calamagrostis nutkaensis PACIFIC REED GRASS
*Eragrostis curvula WEEPING LOVE GRASS
Festuca mairei ATLAS FESCUE
*Leymus arenarius BLUE LYME GRASS
L. condensatus GIANT WILD RYE
Muhlenbergia emersleyi BULL GRASS
M. rigens DEER GRASS
Nassella cernua NODDING NEEDLE GRASS
N. lepida FOOTHILL NEEDLE GRASS
*N. tenuissima MEXICAN FEATHER GRASS
Panicum virgatum SWITCH GRASS
*Pennisetum incomptum MEADOW PENNISETUM
Schizachyrium scoparium LITTLE BLUESTEM
*Sorghastrum nutans INDIAN GRASS
Sporobolus airoides ALKALI DROPSEED
*Vetiveria zizanioides VETIVER

*These plants may become invasive, so check with your local Cooperative Extension Office before purchasing or planting.

Panicum virgatum 'Haense Herms' is one of the best switch grasses for mass planting on a slope. Its handsome leaves are green in summer, turning burgundy in fall, and the whole plant fades to attractive buff tones, as shown, in winter.

Terracing is an age-old method for landscaping a hillside. A variety of colorful drought-tolerant grasses populate this tiered garden in Southern California.

STONES AND BOULDERS

Because they seem to enhance each other's form and texture, stones and grasses make ideal garden partners. The horizontal planes of rocks, boulders, and even stepping-stones act as visual foils for the upright forms of many grasses, and plants with drooping or arching leaves seem to embrace the rocky forms next to them. Grasses' slender blades and delicate flowers make a delightful textural contrast to the hard surface of stones.

In true rock or alpine gardens, compact plants such as common thrift (Armeria maritima), *blue grama* (Bouteloua gracilis), *Pennisetum alopecuroides 'Little Bunny', and smaller fescues add a naturalistic touch, and they won't crowd, or shade nearby plants.*

Against a curtain of horsetail *(Equisetum hyemale),* a stone sculpture rests peacefully on a pillow of mop-headed sedge *(Carex caryophyllea* 'The Beatles').

Repeating a grass throughout a garden helps tie together disparate elements. Without these casually arranged grasses, the rigid lines of concrete and stones would make a harsh intersection.

A single stone holds the center of this colorful composition. Bowles' golden grass *(Carex elata* 'Aurea') mimics a splashing fountain, and its bold color is picked up by the lady's-mantle *(Alchemilla)* in the foreground. To the left of the stone, and emphasizing its vertical form, is Japanese blood grass *(Imperata cylindrica* 'Rubra'); its rich color is matched by the Japanese maple in the upper right-hand corner.

A mature clump of leather leaf sedge *(Carex buchananii)* provides a dramatic focal point where lawn, granite blocks, and flagstone pavers come together. See Chapter 2 for more information on planting among pavers.

Grassy leaves of desert spoon *(Dasylirion wheeleri)* mirror the blue-gray shades of nearby stones in a dry garden. This southwestern native grows slowly to form a spherical clump at least 5 feet wide.

Hard fescue *(Festuca longifolia)* is a tough, low-maintenance grass that can take even dry, shady conditions. Planted between large, irregular stepping-stones, it forms a rugged carpet for this modern outdoor dining area.

IN THE ASIAN STYLE

Some of the most popular landscaping grasses and grasslike plants in American gardens today, including many Carex *and* Miscanthus *species, are from China and Japan. But these plants won't give a garden an authentic Asian look any more than if you simply plunk down a Japanese lantern. Japanese and Chinese gardens seek to capture the spirit of nature—and particularly of the local environs—simply and elegantly. Paths, lanterns, and water features are placed for function first (even if only implied or symbolic); and stone, the very stuff of the earth, is almost always included. Enclosure within a fence, wall, or hedge is also important for Asian-style gardens; this gives them the feel of a peaceful retreat.*

A restrained palette and naturalistic design heighten the quiet drama of this backyard garden. The gray tones of the faded wood deck are picked up in the fieldstone edging and in the fescue's blue-gray leaves. Instead of bright flowers, a single clump of purple fountain grass *(Pennisetum setaceum* 'Rubrum') is used as a color accent.

Sasa veitchii

FOUNTAIN GRASS
Pennisetum orientale

BLACK MONDO GRASS
Ophiopogon planiscapus
'Nigrescens'

DWARF MONDO GRASS
Ophiopogon japonicus
'Kyoto Dwarf'

The dense foliage of golden bamboo *(Phyllostachys aurea)* makes it an excellent choice for a hedge or screen. Low ground covers help conceal containment barriers.

The delicate, fresh green leaves of black bamboo *(Phyllostachys nigra)* contrast beautifully with its dark stems. Like most bamboos, this one sways in the breeze, creating a symphony of rustling leaves and tapping stems.

BAMBOO IN THE GARDEN

Bamboos range from just a few inches to more than 100 feet tall—truly the giants of the grass family. Some of these graceful evergreen plants stay relatively compact; others can spread vigorously to create large groves. Their diversity in size, form, and color makes bamboos the most versatile of grasses—useful as accents, ground covers, hedges, and container plants.

HOW BAMBOO GROWS

At least 1,000 bamboo species have been identified, but they generally fall into one of two categories based on the way their underground stems grow. Clumping types (including *Bambusa, Chusquea, Drepanostachyum, Fargesia,* and *Otatea*) expand slowly and are relatively easy to keep within bounds. They can be used as shrubs, hedges, or accents, and rarely spread beyond their allotted space.

Running types (including *Chimonobambusa, Indocalamus, Phyllostachys, Pleioblastus, Pseudosasa, Sasa, Semiarundinaria,* and *Shibataea*) send out aggressive shoots in every direction. If their spread is contained, the smaller species make excellent ground covers, and the larger ones can be used in the garden like the clumping types. Plant them in a parking strip, in a raised bed surrounded by concrete, or inside a buried plastic or metal barrier. Buried containers should extend 1 to 3 feet in depth, depending on the ultimate size of the plant (see page 115); large nursery containers or trash cans with the bottom cut out also work well. Another way to limit the spread of running bamboos is to insert a spade around the edges of the patch periodically to cut off the spreading shoots.

WHAT BAMBOO NEEDS

Bamboos grow best in moist, organically enriched soil that drains well. Many do well in dappled shade, and most resent hot, dry situations in full sun. In cold areas, they should be planted in spring soon after the last frost; in warmer regions, fall is a good planting time. Water deeply and not too frequently, never letting the soil dry out completely, and apply a balanced fertilizer high in nitrogen to speed growth. Bamboos take a few years to reach their full potential, so be patient. Smaller species make great container plants, where they perform best with their roots confined (see page 105). Standard potting soil and occasional feeding will ensure vigorous growth of container specimens, which can be brought indoors for short periods of time.

Strong, vigorous grower or dangerous, aggressive spreader? Planted next to wide concrete steps, even the rampant *Pleioblastus viridistriatus* is stopped in its tracks, forming a lush mass to 2 feet tall. As long as the running nature of such bamboos is taken into account, there's nothing to fear from them in your garden.

PATIO AND DECK

Not every gardener is blessed with a spacious property. But a patio or deck—even a small balcony—can become a pleasing refuge when filled with thoughtfully designed containers. Start by evaluating the site's exposure; when grown in containers, even the most heat-tolerant plants appreciate some shade and shelter from winds. Grasses grow quickly, so keep their mature size in mind when choosing containers, and place them where watering will be convenient (if potted grasses do dry out, cut them back to spur new growth).

Combine grasses with annuals and perennials, or plant them individually in containers that complement their form and color (see pages 100 to 105). Container choices are almost limitless; in addition to the vast array of pots, urns, boxes, and barrels available at garden centers there are plenty of other objects suitable for holding plants—just make sure they drain well and are roomy enough for the plant's roots. Arrange containers in small groups, placing a few smaller pots around a larger one, for instance, and vary the height by setting small pots on low tables, bricks, or upturned empty pots. Don't hesitate to move pots around until you achieve just the right look—that flexibility is a major benefit of container gardening.

A bowl-shaped pot is the perfect home for a low, clumping grass.

Bold-leafed *Cordyline* and *Phormium* add zest to a collection of unusual containers and objects artfully arranged to reflect the gardener's personal style.

Contain potentially invasive grasses like blue lyme grass *(Leymus arenarius)* (the large blue grass shown here) to enjoy their exuberance without worrying about their spreading. Repeating the urn shape in the two groupings unifies the design.

Mexican feather grass *(Nassella tenuissima)* cascades from a tailored terra-cotta pot at the edge of a wooden deck. Its threadlike foliage and wispy blooms contrast beautifully with the broadleafed plants nearby.

ROOFTOP REFUGE

A flat rooftop affords the urban gardener an opportunity to create a private haven while helping the environment. "Green roofs," based on ancient sod roofs, hold a layer of garden soil planted with shallow-rooted grasses, succulents, or wildflowers. A planted roof provides insulation, reduces storm runoff, and may lower ambient temperatures, reducing energy costs.

A rooftop container garden has many of the same benefits as a green roof but is considerably easier to create. First, make sure that the roof is structurally sound and waterproof—a consultation with an engineer or building inspector may be necessary. Lightweight containers are best, and plants must be tough enough to withstand sun, wind, and temperature extremes. A sturdy trellis or screen can provide shelter for plants and gardeners alike.

This garden in the sky features a screen of feather reed grass *(Calamagrostis × acutiflora)* in lightweight wooden planters behind an urn overflowing with a fountain grass. These are just two of the many grasses sturdy enough for rooftop conditions.

CUTTING GARDENS

Imagine a long-lasting arrangement of delicate flowers mixed with leaves of various sizes and colors, and accented with unusual seeds and pods. Such an arrangement can be gathered entirely from your own cutting garden of grasses.

The steps are the same as for most cut-flower beds. Choose a site with full sun, then turn the soil, adding organic matter such as compost to improve aeration and fertility. Lay out the beds so that flowers will be easy to reach without crushing neighboring plants. For a long season of cut flowers, choose a variety of cool-season and warm-season grasses from the lists on the facing page. Plant annuals from seed after the last frost; set out perennials in spring or fall from nursery containers or plugs. A thick layer of mulch will keep the moisture in and weeds out—but don't crowd it around the stems of young plants.

The abundant blades of grasses can be harvested anytime. Cut the flowers just as they are expanding; they may fall apart if cut when fully open. Enjoy them in vases of water, or dry them in a cool, dark room for one to two weeks.

Majestic flowers of fall-blooming feather reed grass *(Calamagrostis brachytricha)* emerge a striking purple-red in fall, then slowly fade through golden tones to a silvery gray; they are lovely in fresh or dried arrangements.

Bear grass *(Xerophyllum tenax)* is not a grass at all, but an evergreen grassy perennial native to the American West. Its long, slender leaves are familiar in florists' arrangements. Other grassy plants with foliage excellent for cutting are horsetail *(Equisetum hyemale)*, *Miscanthus* species, sugarcane *(Saccharum officinarum)*, and zebra bulrush *(Schoenoplectus tabernaemontani* 'Zebrinus').

Aglow with the setting sun are two annual grasses prized for their flowers: hare's tail grass and foxtail barley.

GRASSES FOR A CUTTING GARDEN

Spring flowering (cool-season growers)

Achnatherum calamagrostis SILVER SPIKE GRASS
Briza media COMMON QUAKING GRASS
Calamagrostis REED GRASS
Carex nudata CALIFORNIA BLACK-FLOWERING SEDGE
C. pseudocyperus CYPERUS SEDGE
Cortaderia selloana PAMPAS GRASS
Cyperus alternifolius UMBRELLA PLANT
Deschampsia cespitosa TUFTED HAIR GRASS
D. flexuosa CRINKLED HAIR GRASS
Elymus canadensis CANADA WILD RYE
Holcus lanatus YORKSHIRE FOG
Hordeum jubatum FOXTAIL BARLEY
Hystrix patula BOTTLEBRUSH GRASS
Luzula WOODRUSH
Melica ciliata HAIRY MELIC GRASS
Milium effusum 'Aureum' GOLDEN WOOD MILLET
Molinia caerulea MOOR GRASS
Nassella tenuissima MEXICAN FEATHER GRASS
Stipa gigantea GIANT FEATHER GRASS

Summer-to-fall flowering
(warm-season growers)

Andropogon gerardii BIG BLUESTEM
A. glomeratus BUSHY BEARD GRASS
A. ternarius SPLIT-BEARD BROOM SEDGE
Arundo donax GIANT REED
Bouteloua gracilis BLUE GRAMA
Carex baccans CRIMSON-SEEDED SEDGE
C. pendula GREAT DROOPING SEDGE
Chasmanthium latifolium WILD OATS
Coix lacryma-jobi JOB'S TEARS
Eragrostis spectabilis PURPLE LOVE GRASS
E. trichodes SAND LOVE GRASS
Erianthus contortus BENT AWN PLUME GRASS
Lagurus ovatus HARE'S TAIL GRASS
Leymus condensatus GIANT WILD RYE
Miscanthus sinensis
Panicum virgatum SWITCH GRASS
Pennisetum FOUNTAIN GRASS
Rhynchelytrum RUBY GRASS
Schizachyrium scoparium LITTLE BLUESTEM
Sorghastrum nutans INDIAN GRASS
Stipa capillata FEATHER GRASS
Tridens flavus PURPLETOP
Typha CATTAIL

This cutting garden comprises various sizes and types of fall flowers. Bunches of fine-textured Mexican feather grass, in the foreground, can be cut before the seeds begin to scatter. Above that are several cultivars of *Miscanthus sinensis* with varied flowers heads that range from reddish to silver.

WINTER INTEREST

Ornamental grasses add loveliness to the garden in every season. Cool-season growers flower in spring, while warm-season types save their blossoms for summer and fall. But winter may be the most dramatic season of all for these adaptable plants. The imposing skeletons of many large grasses, bleached in dormancy to tones of sandy beige, remain upright when other garden plants have given up the ghost. Fine-leafed grasses, such as feather reed grass and switch grass, are good choices for winter gardens; snow slips off their narrow leaves rather then weighing them down. And sturdy players like little bluestem and ravenna grass stand up to snow and wind, offering food and shelter to birds and small animals. The colors of evergreen grasses such as leather-leaf sedge and blue oat grass are even more stunning against a backdrop of snow.

Native to vast stretches of the North American prairie, big bluestem is unfazed by the rigors of winter. The buff tones of many dormant grasses stand out particularly well against a dark background or where they'll catch the sun's rays from the side or behind.

Like icing on the cake of this classic planting scheme, frost tops the rounded flower heads of *Sedum* 'Autumn Joy' backed by spiky blooms of fountain grass.

THEY LAUGH AT THE COLD

The grasses listed below show little or no damage after exposure to temperatures as low as –30°F; those marked with an asterisk are extremely cold-tolerant, surviving down to –40°F. A protective layer of mulch helps any grass through the coldest months.

Acorus calamus SWEET FLAG
Alopecurus pratensis 'Aureus' YELLOW FOXTAIL GRASS
*Andropogon gerardii BIG BLUESTEM
A. virginicus BROOM SEDGE
*Arrhenatherum elatius bulbosum 'Variegatum' STRIPED BULBOUS OAT GRASS
*Bouteloua curtipendula SIDE-OATS GRAMA
*B. gracilis BLUE GRAMA
*Bromus inermis 'Skinner's Gold'
*Buchloe dactyloides BUFFALO GRASS
*Calamagrostis × acutiflora 'Karl Foerster' KARL FOERSTER FEATHER REED GRASS
C. × acutiflora 'Overdam' VARIEGATED FEATHER REED GRASS

*C. brachytricha FALL-BLOOMING FEATHER REED GRASS
Carex digitata FINGERED SEDGE
*C. flacca BLUE SEDGE
C. flava YELLOW SEDGE
*C. grayi GRAY'S SEDGE
C. montana MOUNTAIN SEDGE
*C. muskingumensis PALM SEDGE
C. nigra BLACK-FLOWERING SEDGE
C. speciosa 'Velebit Humilis' VELVET SEDGE
C. stricta TUSSOCK SEDGE
C. umbrosa UMBROSA SEDGE
*Deschampsia cespitosa TUFTED HAIR GRASS
D. flexuosa CRINKLED HAIR GRASS
*Elymus canadensis CANADA WILD RYE
*Eriophorum angustifolium COTTON GRASS
Festuca amethystina LARGE BLUE FESCUE
*F. glauca BLUE FESCUE
F. muelleri MUELLER'S FESCUE
F. tenuifolia FINE-LEAFED FESCUE
Hakonechloa macra JAPANESE FOREST GRASS
*Helictotrichon sempervirens BLUE OAT GRASS
Hystrix patula BOTTLEBRUSH GRASS
*Juncus effusus SOFT RUSH

Koeleria brevis BLUE HAIR GRASS
*Leymus arenarius BLUE LYME GRASS
Luzula sylvatica GREATER WOODRUSH
*Miscanthus 'Giganteus' GIANT SILVER GRASS
M. oligostachyus SMALL JAPANESE SILVER GRASS
*M. sacchariflorus CHINESE SILVER GRASS
*M. sinensis 'Purpurascens' FLAME GRASS
*M. s. 'Silberfeder' SILVER FEATHER MISCANTHUS
M. s. 'Variegatus'
*Molinia caerulea arundinacea TALL PURPLE MOOR GRASS
*M. c. 'Variegata' VARIEGATED MOOR GRASS
*Panicum virgatum SWITCH GRASS
Pennisetum flaccidum MEADOW PENNISETUM
*Phalaris arundinacea 'Feesey' RIBBON GRASS
*Schizachyrium scoparium LITTLE BLUESTEM
Sesleria caerulea BLUE MOOR GRASS
S. heufleriana BLUE-GREEN MOOR GRASS
S. nitida GRAY MOOR GRASS
*Sorghastrum nutans INDIAN GRASS
*Spartina pectinata PRAIRIE CORD GRASS
Spodiopogon sibericus SIBERIAN GRAYBEARD
*Sporobolus heterolepis PRAIRIE DROPSEED
Themeda japonica THEMEDA

Their colors muted, grasses' bold forms are even more evident in winter. Dormant flowers of miscanthus hold snow without being crushed by it, and feather reed grass stands cleanly upright in the background.

Black bamboo (*Phyllostachys nigra*) is dramatic in the snow. Because they are evergreen, bamboos are an excellent source of color in the winter garden, but the hardiest can survive only to about –20°F.

T

IN AND OUT OF
E GARDEN

Throughout the pages of this book, you've seen plenty of ways in which grasses fit into the garden—from meadows to privacy screens. But the beauty and utility of grasses don't stop when they are out of the ground. In fact, there is a multitide of other ways to use grasses and bamboos around your home. For instance, grasses add a fine, often airy texture to container plantings. In fact, when it comes to great grasses for containers, your main challenge will be deciding which among the many to choose. And what do you do with the grassy clippings from your cutting garden (see pages 94–95)? Use them to fill vases in the house, for starters. Finally, utilitarian bamboo is strong enough to use in clever do-it-yourself projects. There are a few to get you started on page 111.

Planting and caring for the ornamental grasses in your garden should be easy. All they really need is sun, water, and soil. Like other green plants, they make their own food. Whether or not you decide to supplement their natural growth with fertilizers is largely a matter of choice. But all grasses need to be groomed occasionally to keep them looking their best.

There are few pests and only one disease that prey on ornamental grasses. In fact, most problems associated with these plants can be avoided with a little planning and forethought. On pages 120 to 121 you'll find a few tips to help you with the most troubling situations.

Potted grasses reminiscent of those that cover California's foothills in summer include, at left, *Pennisetum setaceum* 'Rubrum' with blue *Salvia sinaloensis,* and on the right, *Miscanthus sinensis* 'Yaku Jima' with *Scaevola aemula* 'New Wonder'.

SINGULARLY DRAMATIC

A simple emphasis beside a wooden bench, this egg-plant-colored grass stands out against a background of bamboo.

Weeping brown New Zealand sedge *(Carex flagillifera)* has narrow pendent bronze leaves that drape appealingly over the sides of its container.

It's easy to see how *Miscanthus sinensis* 'Purpurascens' gets its common name, flame grass. In October these container specimens are ablaze with color.

Japanese forest grass *(Hakonechloa macra* 'Aure-ola') will light up a dark corner of the patio or deck, but its true color depends on the amount of sun it receives. In cooler climates, the leaves will be paler in their variegation but compensate by blushing pink and crimson in fall.

Grasslike *Agave stricta* does not invite handling—its 2-foot-long stems are tipped with prickly spines. In a container, however, it is quite harmless.

Free-sowing *Nassella tenuissima* is another favorite container subject. In this case, the intrepid blond-maned grass grew on its own, lodging amid some ivy geraniums. In bloom, Mexican feather grass is as showy as any flower.

New Zealand flax is one of the most popular container subjects. Not only does it respond well to pot culture, but the stiff leaves can be as dramatic as any architectural element or sculpture. Here, it is paired with Pride of Madeira beside a Mediterranean-style swimming pool.

Mingling together in a gracious urn, flowering maple *(Abutilon)* and New Zealand hair sedge *(Carex comans)* create a subtle combination of peach and pale burgundy.

At Wave Hill botanical garden in New York, a pair of pots with a spiky cordyline and *Hakonechloa macra* 'Aureola' are a contrast in texture, height, and color.

COLORFUL COMBINATIONS

This Indonesian basket is hung with rough hemp rope and filled by Mark Bartos to overflowing with plants of various foliage textures and colors. They include *Agapanthus* 'Dark Star', *Juncus* 'Oaxaca', *Acalypha wilkesiana, Acorus gramineus* 'Ogon', *Russelia equisetiformis, Cordyline australis* 'Albertii', and *Crocosmia*.

This bountiful mixture of tender grasses includes *Pennisetum setaceum* 'Rubrum', *Setaria palmifolia* 'Variegata', and pink-tipped *Rhynchelytrum repens*.

Beautiful *Pennisetum villosum* has charming fuzzy flower heads that are paired here with the more wispy flowers of switch grass *(Panicum virgatum)* and free-flowering cosmos.

A design by Oehme and Van Sweden features some signature favorites, such as *Pennisetum setaceum* 'Rubrum' and gray artemisia.

You can have a pond in a pot. This simple tub is placed on a deck and filled with *Carex morrowii* 'Variegata', wider-leafed *Phalaris arundinacea, Xanthosoma sagittifolium,* and *X. violaceum.*

Create a miniature meadow. This Montana big sky summer arrangement contains blue oat grass *(Helictotrichon sempervirens), Coreopsis verticillata* 'Moonbeam', dwarf Shasta daisy, *Verbascum bombyciferum* 'Arctic Summer', *Verbena bonariensis,* and yellow yarrow.

Maiden grass is the main attraction in this arrangement by Juanita Nye. Surrounding it are *Helichrysum* 'Bright Orange Bikini', *Bidens ferulifolia,* pineapple mint, and calendulas.

In August a wheelbarrow backed by fountain grass and yarrow in Golden, Colorado, is filled with blooming daylilies, golden coreopsis, purple liatris, and *Sedum* 'Vera Jameson'.

'Paper White' narcissus grow through a meadow of winter rye. The bulbs were planted first, then grass seeds were sown on top.

DARINGLY DIFFERENT

Containers don't have to be filled, nor furniture occupied. Here, an empty urn and a graceful chair are adrift in a sea of Mexican feather grass.

Contain your bamboo if you are afraid it will get out of hand. Then double it up with a well-placed mirror and surround it with sculpture.

For indoors or out, *Scirpus cernuus* grows happily in a glass cube filled with white gravel.

This tropical mixture includes *Canna* 'Tropicanna', *Begonia* 'Flame Orange', flowering maple, *Lotus maculatus* 'Gold Flash', shell ginger *(Alpinia zerumbet* 'Variegata'), acorus, bromeliads, croton, and *Cordyline stricta*.

CONTAINER CARE

Grasses require less maintenance than many other container plants. Most do well in any pot of ample size. While they aren't fussy about soil, they thrive in a rich container mix that provides good drainage. Although many grasses tolerate drier conditions than other plants, they can't stand going bone-dry. If that happens and the plants go brown, cut them back to encourage new growth.

Feed potted grasses twice monthly during the growing season with a high-nitrogen liquid fertilizer diluted to half strength. You'll need to cut back most grasses in late winter or early spring, after their foliage has browned. Evergreen types may need just occasional grooming or combing to remove dead leaves. About every three years, knock plants out of their pots, cut the clumps in halves or quarters, and replant the divisions, discarding the parts of the clumps (usually the centers) that have died out.

In cold-winter areas, nonhardy grasses can be grown as annuals. *Pennisetum setaceum* 'Rubrum' is a favorite tender container subject. In the hot-summer areas of California and the Southwest, grasses that like a cool, moist climate can be grown as three-season plants, from fall to early spring.

Grasses must be well drained; it's an absolute requirement. This assortment of pot "feet" and supports keep the containers off the ground so they can drain freely.

BAMBOOS INDOORS

Elegant as Japanese brush paintings and strong as wood, bamboo makes as remarkable a house plant as it does a garden subject. Put the plants in suitably large pots and set them against plain walls or windows—bamboos will grow anywhere as long as they get enough light and moisture. Keep the potting soil moist, and regularly mist the plants to compensate for the lack of humidity found indoors. To guarantee they'll stay in bounds, select from among the favorites listed here, or ask your vendor for others that are sure small-scale bets.

To restrain your bamboo further, allow the roots to become pot-bound. This isn't a good practice for most plants, but it's fine for bamboo, containing the growth of both running and clumping types. And as bamboo tend to be heavy feeders, you can also restrict growth by applying controlled-release fertilizer every four months, beginning when new growth starts.

Bamboo culms emerge from the soil with the same diameter they'll have when they're grown; break off the large culms but let the smaller ones grow to keep the texture of the plant in scale with an indoor setting.

New leaves can appear in any of three seasons, depending on the type of bamboo. As new leaves grow, old leaves fall off. This is the messiest time for bamboos; set them outdoors if the weather allows. If your bamboo regularly loses its leaves, it may be having trouble adjusting to its situation; try placing the pot in a different site, letting the plant spend some time out of doors in mild weather, and keeping humidity levels high.

TEN HOUSE-BOUND BAMBOOS

High Light (6 hours or more light per day)
Arundinaria anceps 'Pitt White'
Bambusa ventricosa BUDDHA'S BELLY BAMBOO
Otatea acuminata aztecorum MEXICAN WEEPING BAMBOO

Moderate Light (4 to 6 hours per day)
Chimonobambusa marmorea MARBLED BAMBOO
Pleioblastus chino murakamianus GINTAI-AZUMANEZA

Low Light (less than 4 hours per day)
Hibanobambusa tranquillans 'Shiroshima'
Indocalamus tessellata BIG-LEAFED BAMBOO
Pleioblastus shibuyanus 'Tsuboi'
P. variegata DWARF WHITESTRIPE BAMBOO
Sasaella masumuneana albostriata

Growing gracefully in ornate containers, these three bamboos are, from left, *Sasaella masumuneana albostriata, Gintai-azumaneza,* and *Arundinaria anceps* 'Pitt White'.

GOOD FOR POTS

In addition to the plants shown here, the following also make good container subjects.

Green Foliage
Calamagrostis × acutiflora FEATHER REED GRASS
Chasmanthium latifolium WILD OATS
Chondropetalum tectorum CAPE RUSH
Cortaderia selloana 'Pumila' COMPACT PAMPAS GRASS
Elegia capensis BROOM REED
Pennisetum alopecuroides 'Hameln' DWARF FOUNTAIN GRASS
P. orientale FOUNTAIN GRASS
Stipa arundinacea FEATHER GRASS
Restio festucaeformis

Blue Foliage
Leymus arenarius BLUE LYME GRASS
Paspalum quadrifolia

Silver Foliage
Miscanthus sinensis 'Morning Light' JAPANESE SILVER GRASS

Yellow Foliage
Carex oshimensis 'Evergold' VARIEGATED JAPANESE SEDGE

C. nudata CALIFORNIA BLACK-FLOWERING SEDGE
Miscanthus sinensis 'Hinjo'
Molinia caerulea 'Variegata' VARIEGATED MOOR GRASS
Muhlenbergia dumosa BAMBOO MUHLY

Red Foliage or Flowers
Imperata cylindrica 'Rubra' JAPANESE BLOOD GRASS
Panicum virgatum 'Haense Herms' and 'Shenandoah' (FALL COLOR)
Pennisetum alopecuroides 'Moudry'
P. 'Burgundy Giant'
Saccharum officinarum 'Pele's Smoke'
Uncinia rubra RED HOOK SEDGE
Vetiveria zizanioides VETIVER (FALL COLOR)

Moisture Lovers
Carex elata 'Aurea'
Cyperus (MANY)
Equisetum hyemale HORSETAIL
Juncus (MANY)
Typha CATTAIL

ARRANGING GRASSES

ASIAN-STYLE ARRANGEMENT

From feng shui to tonsus, Asian themes and furnishings are popular in American homes. The key to a successful display? Simplicity. Set in this rectangular porcelain base are three basic elements: bamboo, horsetail, and a potted 4-inch scirpus.

OTHER ASIAN GRASSES

Upright

Equisetum hyemale HORSETAIL
Phyllostachys nigra BLACK BAMBOO
Saccharum officinarum 'Pele's Smoke'
  PURPLE-STEMMED SUGARCANE
Schoenoplectus tabernaemontani 'Zebrinus'
  ZEBRA BULRUSH

Potted

Acorus gramineus 'Pusillus' DWARF JAPANESE
  SWEET FLAG
Equisetum contorta MINIATURE CONTORTED
  HORSETAIL
Festuca glauca 'Blaufink' BLUEFINCH FESCUE
F. glauca 'Elijah Blue'
Sesleria heufleriana BLUE-GREEN MOOR GRASS
Uncinia rubra RED HOOK SEDGE

Flame grass (*Miscanthus sinensis* 'Purpurascens')

WHIMSICAL WOMAN

Like Carmen Miranda, this humorous vase sports a fanciful headdress of nature's bounty. It includes feather grass, bear grass, green miniature cymbidium orchids, and a fringe of papyrus.

OTHER PLAYFUL GRASSES

Andropogon ternarius SPLIT-BEARD
  BROOM SEDGE
Carex grayi GRAY'S SEDGE
C. pendula 'Moonraker' GREAT DROOPING
  SEDGE
Chionochloa rubra SNOW GRASS
Cortaderia selloana PAMPAS GRASS
Eriophorum latifolium BROAD-LEAFED
  COTTON GRASS
Juncus effusus 'Spiralis' CORKSCREW RUSH
Pennisetum villosum FEATHERTOP

COOLLY CONTEMPORARY

A modern glass vase and a few dramatic leaves are all that are needed to create an up-to-date grassy setting. A knot or two tied into these New Zealand flax *(Phormium tenax)* leaves create a surprising double-take.

OTHER MODERN GRASSES

Chondropetalum tectorum CAPE RUSH
Cortaderia selloana 'Pumila' COMPACT PAMPAS GRASS
Cyperus alternifolius UMBRELLA PLANT
Panicum virgatum 'Warrior' 'WARRIOR' SWITCH GRASS
Spartina pectinata 'Aureomarginata'
  GOLDEN-EDGED PRAIRIE CORD GRASS
Tripsacum dactyloides EASTERN GAMA GRASS
Typha minima MINIATURE CATTAIL
Yucca flaccida 'Golden Sword'

ROSES FOR ROMANCE

Softening the contours of a rose arrangement and adding subtle texture and color, grasses enhance an old-fashioned display. This Victorian jug is filled with 'Perfume Delight' roses and fountain grass *(Pennisetum setaceum)*.

OTHER ROMANTIC GRASSES

Achnatherum speciosum INDIAN RICE GRASS
Briza maxima and *B. media* QUAKING GRASS
Carex baccans CRIMSON-SEEDED SEDGE
C. nudata CALIFORNIA BLACK-FLOWERING SEDGE
Cymbopogon citratus LEMON GRASS
Deschampsia flexuosa CRINKLED HAIR GRASS
Eragrostis spectabilis PURPLE LOVE GRASS
Luzula nivea SNOWY WOODRUSH
Melica altissima SIBERIAN MELIC 'ALBA' (WHITE) OR
    'ATROPURPUREA' (PURPLE)
Muhlenbergia filipes GULF MUHLY
Rhynchelytrum repens RUBY GRASS
Tridens flavus PURPLETOP

OUTDOORS IN

Nestled in a tight spiral bouquet, these long-lasting grassy flowers and durable foliage include fountain grass *(Pennisetum alopecuroides)*, miscanthus, Japanese blood grass, wild oats *(Chasmanthium latifolium)*, hare's tail grass *(Lagurus ovatus)*, feather grass *(Stipa)*, and weeping love grass *(Eragrostis curvula)*.

OTHER NATURALISTIC GRASSES

Alopecurus pratensis 'Variegatus'
    GOLDEN MEADOW FOXTAIL
Andropogon gerardii BIG BLUESTEM
Bouteloua gracilis BLUE GRAMA
Calamagrostis REED GRASS
Hordeum jubatum FOXTAIL BARLEY
Koeleria macrantha JUNE GRASS
Melica ciliata HAIRY MELIC GRASS
Molinia caerulea 'Moorhexe' MOOR GRASS
M. c. 'Strahlenquelle'
Panicum virgatum SWITCH GRASS
Schizachyrium scoparium LITTLE BLUESTEM
Spodiopogon sibericus SIBERIAN GRAYBEARD

Wild oats *(Chasmanthium latifolium)*

A DRAMATIC TOUCH

What better way to bring the feeling of the outdoors into your living room than to fill a large vase to overflowing with plants from meadow and streamside? This exuberant mix includes porcupine grass *(Miscanthus sinensis* 'Strictus'), cattails *(Typha latifolia)*, hair grass *(Deschampsia)*, bear grass, and montbretia.

OTHER DRAMATIC GRASSES

Arundo donax GIANT REED
Cyperus isocladus DWARF PAPYRUS
Helictotrichon sempervirens BLUE OAT GRASS
Imperata cylindrica 'Rubra' JAPANESE
  BLOOD GRASS
Miscanthus sinensis 'Silberfeder' SILVERFEATHER
  MISCANTHUS
Phalaris arundinacea 'Feesey' FEESEY'S
  RIBBON GRASS
Saccharum giganteum and *S. ravennae*
  SUGARCANE
Vetiveria zizanioides VETIVER

Zebra grass *(Miscanthus sinensis* 'Zebrinus')

Bamboo fencing and trellises

Part of the appeal of bamboo is that it looks both strong and delicate at once. So a fence of mixed bamboo panels and crosspieces, with a large circular cutout, gracefully links two sides of the garden.

An intricate screen acts as a divider for this quiet corner. In the center, a bamboo fountain splashes into a hollowed rock. Similar fencing and fountain materials are available through many garden suppliers.

BAMBOO FENCING

If you grow bamboo in the ground, it won't be long before you are harvesting your own canes. You'll probably put them to use in the garden as plant stakes and supports, bed edgings, or simple structures. By doing so, you are following a centuries-old tradition.

Building bamboo fences—with exotic names like rifle-barrel fence *(Teppo-gaki),* raincoat fence *(Mino-gaki),* and four-eyed fence *(Yotsume-gaki)*—is an ancient practice in Japan and other Asian countries. That only makes sense, given the plentiful natural supplies of this inexpensive, sturdy, and strong material.

Now the same is available to consumers in the West. Bamboo is becoming widely available, both as single canes and as premade panels for fencing, gates, pergolas, privacy screens, and a wide variety of decorative items for both indoors and out. You can find suppliers for some of these items on pages 126 to 127. In terms of style, bamboo fencing and other structures are probably most at home in Asian, woodland, and naturalistic-themed gardens, but if you grow fruits and vegetables, you'll find the bamboo trellises shown here to be indispensable.

TRELLISES AND TEPEES

Kids love places in which to hide, and plants need support as they grow. Combine the two, and you have the traditional tepee shape used by gardeners the world over. Bamboo is the perfect material for constructing plant supports; all you need is a saw, a drill, and hemp twine for lashing canes together.

Half-rounds of bamboo lashed together make a stockade-like barrier, fronted by low-growing grasses. A similar technique can be used to disguise an unsightly chain-link fence.

The simplest kind of tepee, just four bamboo poles wired or tied together at the top, provides enough support for climbing beans or peas.

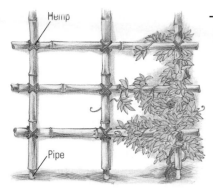

Hemp

Pipe

MAKING A BAMBOO TRELLIS

The bamboo poles available in lengths of 4 to 12 feet from many nurseries and mail-order sources are a surprisingly strong and durable material for a fence, and of course, much lighter in weight than lumber. For a large fence, choose 1½-inch bamboo poles; for a small one, you might use ¾-inch poles. Avoid using the "split" or "half-round" bamboo for support pieces; they're not as durable.

To make the simple fencing shown here, lay out the horizontal crosspieces at even intervals on a flat surface. Then place the vertical poles so they alternate in front of and behind the crosspieces. Bind the poles where they cross, using either 15-gauge copper wire or precut pieces of galvanized wire (available from bamboo suppliers). Feed the wire through oversize pilot holes drilled all the way through both pieces, then twist the ends together at the back with a pair of sturdy pliers. Be sure to wear gloves to protect your hands. For a traditional Japanese look, cover the wire with decorative hemp. To make the trellis less open, weave split bamboo or slim bundles of bamboo branches between the poles.

Because bamboo poles will rot when the ends are buried, slip the trellis poles over pipes set in the soil (the bamboo's solid internodes will keep the poles from sliding down the pipes), or suspend the trellis between cedar, redwood, or pressure-treated posts. Cut the tops of the poles just above an internode or cap them, so rain won't collect in them.

A lattice of espaliered dwarf apples is made here in a modified "Belgian fence," in which branches cross to form diamonds. The diamonds measure about 2 feet on each side, allowing plenty of air circulation.

BEAN TEPEE

To make the leafy tepee shown here takes only about a hour. You'll need six bamboo poles, 8 feet long and 1 inch in diameter; about 60 feet of sturdy hemp or jute twine; and 80 feet of ⅛-inch-diameter clothesline rope.

Line up the poles on the ground, alternating thick and thin ends. Fasten a 10-foot length of twine to the first pole by tying a sturdy hitch or knot. Loop the twine loosely around six poles three or four times (right top).

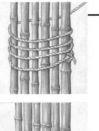

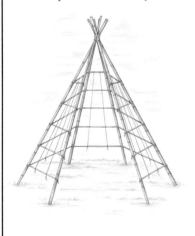

Secure the loops by binding twine around them at right angles, weaving it between the poles (right bottom). At the final pole, fasten off the binding by tying a hitch or knot. Pick up the poles and spread them in a circle about 8 feet across. Allow extra space between the two poles that will frame the entrance.

String clothesline horizontally around the tepee at 1-foot intervals (left). As you work, wrap the clothesline once around each pole and give it a tug to take up the slack. To complete the grid, attach two or three lengths of twine vertically to the clothesline between support poles.

Shopping for Grasses

Retail nurseries are offering greater numbers of ornamental grasses these days. One advantage of buying retail is that you can often see the plants in bloom.

As with any new planting, it's best to do a little preparation before you actually purchase grasses for your garden. First, consider the limits and advantages of your particular zone or microclimate. Factor in the ultimate size and proper spacing of the grasses you are considering. If you live in an arid climate, how will you irrigate your meadow? Will you fertilize? Will you put in plants or seed? Lots of grasses that are not recommended for your area might do fine with some extra assistance. But be realistic about how much time you have to spend caring for your garden.

There are several ways to find the choicest ornamental grasses. You can begin your search with a walk through a local garden center. Look through this book or consult other ornamental grass resources (see pages 126–127). Send away for some catalogs that specialize in ornamental grasses. Visit gardens and arboretums in your area that feature grasses. Arrange to stop by a wholesale specialty nursery.

Most grasses grow quickly, so for the most economical option buy the smallest plants. You might also inherit a plant or two from someone who is dividing the grasses in his or her garden (see page 119) — but be sure to check all plants you bring into your garden for disease and invasiveness (see pages 120–121).

ORDERING FROM A CATALOG

You will discover that if you send for plant catalogs, you'll receive the ones you requested plus a few more. Catalogs show plants, grown in nurseries throughout the country, that may or may not be available in your local nursery or garden center. Look through all of them—you may find something you like. You can then order by calling a toll-free number in the catalog, filling out the order form included inside, or going to the company's Web site (see "Internet Shopping," facing page). Ordering by telephone is quick, and the sales representative can tell you exactly when the grasses will be shipped, but you will usually have to give your credit card number over the phone (as you will if you order online).

Many nurseries feature display gardens that will both entice and inspire you. At Marcia Dickie's nursery in Boyes Hot Springs, California, 'Robert Youngi' bamboo is planted with an assortment of Japanese maples and conifers.

A much wider variety of grasses and grasslike plants are available to consumers through specialty nurseries. At this wholesale grass nursery, pots and flats of grasses of all descriptions cover the ground. Some wholesalers will let you visit and buy plants, but only by appointment.

If you decide to fill out the order form instead, be sure to add shipping and any necessary sales tax. If your figures are incorrect, someone from the catalog company will send you a letter to help get the order straight. A quick call to a company's customer service number can tell you exactly when your purchase will be shipped (this may depend on the plants' availability or the best time for planting in your area). Once the order is processed, you will receive a box of plants through the mail or a private carrier.

CHOOSING A SEED MIX

If you are planting a meadow, you may want to start with seed, which is also available through specialty nurseries. There are two things to keep in mind when choosing seed: what kind you want and how much to get. Be aware of whether the kind you are looking for is a warm- or cool-season grass (see page 9). Decide if you want a mix of wildflowers or perennials with your grasses. For a more homogeneous planting, look for a product that has a low percentage of weeds (which can also be wildflowers) and crop seeds compared with grass seed. Whatever the final grass texture you are trying to achieve, look for seed with a high germination rate.

To determine how much seed to buy, measure the area to be seeded and figure out the square footage. Most catalogs or sales representatives will be able to tell you the recommended amount of seed per square foot for any given grass. But in general, 1,000 square feet of grass requires 1 pound of seed.

WHEN YOUR PLANTS ARRIVE

Most boxes containing live plant material need to be opened immediately upon arrival. Check your order. Did you receive the kind and number of plants you asked for? Sometimes mix-ups do occur.

Don't be alarmed if your grasses don't look as green as expected. Green plants need air, water, and sunlight to survive—none of these needs were met while the plants were in transit. Water plants that look dry. And because the temperature inside the box they traveled in may have varied greatly, put the grasses in a semishaded spot with mild temperatures. For best results, most live grasses sent through the mail need to be planted as soon as possible. Some might be dormant, but these will be marked and will have instructions about when and how to plant them.

If you ordered a bag of grass seed, open that box upon arrival as well. Check the bag for evidence of moisture. The seed should be dry, with none beginning to sprout. It should not smell of mold or mildew. And as with the live plants, be sure you received the seed you ordered.

INTERNET SHOPPING

If you have a computer with Internet access, you'll find that the Web is a great resource for purchasing grasses. Many plant companies and nurseries have Web sites where you can browse their catalogs online and place orders using a credit card. The Internet is a very busy place—here are a few tips that will make your navigating more fruitful:

- Using one of the large search engines to look for specific plant companies that carry ornamental grasses can take some time. Begin your search with some of the specific Web addresses on pages 126 to 127.
- If you can't find the Web site of a plant company or nursery you've heard of, try typing www.plantcompany.com in your browser's Web-address box (with the company name in place of "plantcompany").
- Use the bookmarks feature in the menu bar at the top of your screen to save the Web sites you are interested in. Then you can revisit them without having to remember or input their Web addresses.
- Once you have begun opening the various pages of a Web site, use the back and forward buttons at the top of the browser window to return to specific pages. And become familiar with your browser's history function, which will provide you with a scrollable list of recently visited sites.

Reputable nurseries in the mail-order business make every effort to deliver fresh, undamaged, nondiseased plants. Most include information about how to transplant your new plants. Some even offer transplanting tips on their Web sites.

Don't be dismayed if your new plants look small. They will grow very quickly, given the right conditions. Some larger grasses, like bamboo, need to be folded to fit into a box. Don't panic! They will generally straighten out in a day or two.

PREPARATION AND PLANTING

Although some grasses do very well in soil that has not been amended at all, it's a good idea to prepare the soil by digging it up and adding organic matter such as humus or compost. Most soils that have been amended will allow plants to drain properly—a crucial requirement for many grasses. If your soil is already a good clay loam, dig in a 2- to 3-inch layer of organic matter. For heavy clay soil, you'll need to add twice that amount. One cubic yard (27 cubic feet) covers 108 square feet with a 3-inch layer. A 2-cubic-foot bag covers 8 square feet 3 inches deep.

PLANTING OPTIONS

Situation	Preparation	Procedure	Notes
Preparing an existing bed	Remove weeds and fertilize individual plants.	1. Pull out weeds by hand. 2. Loosen and amend soil around planting hole. 3. Mix 1 to 2 tablespoons of organic fertilizer with the soil you remove from each hole before putting it back.	Continue to remove weeds. Give newly planted grasses plenty of water.
Preparing an unplanted area (organic)	Smother unwanted vegetation by blocking out sunlight and air.	1. Cover with a sheet of black plastic or overlapping layers of newspaper. 2. If paper, cover with dense mulch, which can be tilled under later.	Can take several months to smother unwanted plants and seeds, but can work as quickly as one week if you use plastic sheet in high temperatures.
Preparing an unplanted area (organic)	Turn over soil to remove weeds. Not a good option for areas with weeds that reproduce with runners.	1. Dig out or cut back weeds. 2. Till under remaining plant material with a spade or machine tiller.	May need to repeat at least three more times (one week apart) to completely kill new generations of weeds.
Preparing an unplanted or planted area (inorganic)	Use a herbicide such as glyphosate to kill existing vegetation—whether weeds or an existing planting. Best for larger areas.	1. Cut back or mow existing plants. 2. Apply herbicide, following the directions on the label. Keep children and pets from area as directed.	Weeds should begin to turn brown in less than ten days. Wait two or three weeks to see if weeds grow back. Apply again as needed.
Preparing a planted area (organic)	Digging up unwanted sod.	1. Remove existing sod with a spade. Dig out small rectangular pieces one at a time, or longer strips and roll them back upon themselves. Alternatively, remove existing sod with a sod cutter. (Available at most home and garden-equipment rental businesses.)	A 5-by-20-foot area can take an afternoon to dig up. The machine detaches strips of sod 18 inches by 3 to 4 feet long. Use sod elsewhere, or add to compost. After sod is removed, treat for weeds using one of the methods given above.

PLANTING PLUGS

Dig a hole for each plant the same depth as its container, and an inch or two wider. If you are planting a bare-root grass, make the hole the length of the roots. For protection against pesky gophers, surround each root ball with ½-inch chicken wire. Or line each planting hole intended for a bare-root grass with a basket of wire.

If there is a matted mass of roots on the outside of the root ball, gently loosen the roots with your fingers. Place each plant in a hole and fill with soil. Be careful to keep the soil level the same as it was in the container. If too much of the root ball is exposed to air, the plant will dry out, and if the crown is buried too deep, the plant will rot. Keep this in mind for bare-root planting as well.

Tamp the soil around each plant, and water. When all grasses have been planted and watered, spread a layer of mulch an inch or two deep throughout the bed—but don't pile up too much mulch around the crowns of the plants.

PLANTING SEEDS

Find out the best time of year to plant your seed in your area. Prepare and level the soil as you would for any other kind of planting, but don't cultivate too finely or it may crust over and new seedlings will have a hard time popping through. Prepare the seed for sowing by mixing it with an extender like sand, vermiculite, or sawdust. This makes it easier to see where you have covered, and light, fluffy seed will be distributed more evenly. A rule of thumb for this mixture is 4 pounds of extender to 1 pound of seed.

Sow the seed mixture by hand on a windless day. Walk back and forth in parallel lines across the area you are planting, scattering the seed with steady and even tosses. Cover the same area again, this time perpendicularly to your first rows. Lightly rake the seeds into the soil, and tamp them into the ground with the flat side of a rake. Gently water the area, and cover with a light mulch of clean oat or wheat straw. Keep the soil moist until the seedlings sprout, then water frequently until the plants become established. Wait to pull out weeds! Be sure you are able to clearly identify what is wanted and not wanted in this area.

Before digging a single hole, arrange the grass plants on the ground. A general rule of thumb for spacing is to plant them as far apart as their potential height at maturity.

PLANTING AND CONTAINING BAMBOO

1 Clumping bamboos spread a few inches at at time with short-necked rhizomes; more invasive running bamboos spread by means of underground runners.

2 Contain running bamboo by planting in containers or completely enclosing the roots with commercial bamboo barrier made of a continuous, impermeable, nondecomposing material.

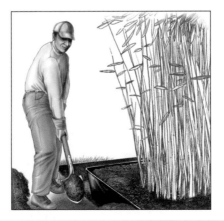

3 Commercial barrier material is available in pieces up to 20 inches. If shoots start to escape the barrier, dig down around the original clump and slice off the shoots at root level.

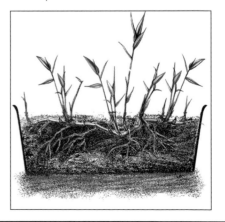

WATERING GRASSES

Emitter line

Emitter line (cutaway view)

How much water do ornamental grasses need? Some climates seem to have the perfect amount of precipitation, and grasses get watered adequately throughout the year without any supplemental irrigation. Other areas, especially in the West and Southwest, are arid, and even drought-tolerant grasses will need some supplemental watering. There are many ways to get water to your plants if you need to, each with its benefits and disadvantages. Whatever system you choose, be sure to be as consistent as possible with the amount of water you give your plants. Many grasses are known for their drought tolerance, but too little or too much water can stress them to a point of no return.

Theories abound on the subject of irrigation, and there are a variety of resources available. To find out more, start with Sunset's *Garden Watering Systems*.

DRIP IRRIGATION COMPONENTS

Most growers of ornamental grasses would agree that an irrigation system that delivers water only to the base of each plant is best. Such a system is referred to as "drip irrigation," or low-flow and volume watering. When you place drip tubes of laser line, emitter-embedded line, or soaker hose next to your grass plants, water soaks in where the plants' roots will benefit most, away from unplanted areas and off the foliage and flowers of surrounding plants.

Along with the benefits of drip irrigation, there are several problems associated with it. If your water is hard (which means it contains an excess of minerals and salts), the tiny holes in laser line can become clogged. Fibrous roots can also plug them up. (Using line with embedded emitters and a root-inhibiting product can sometimes solve the plugging problem.) But no drip lines are safe from gophers, pets, and people disturbing them, as they are thin and easily moved or chewed through. If the line is covered with mulch, you may not notice any watering disruption until it is too late.

Probably the biggest drawback to drip irrigation for ornamental grasses is the impracticality of using it to water a big lawn or meadow. Rather than running many lines and emitters to every plant, it might be simpler to have several overhead sprinklers covering the same area.

Timer

Backflow preventer

Filter

Pressure regulator

Compression fitting

Micro-sprinklers

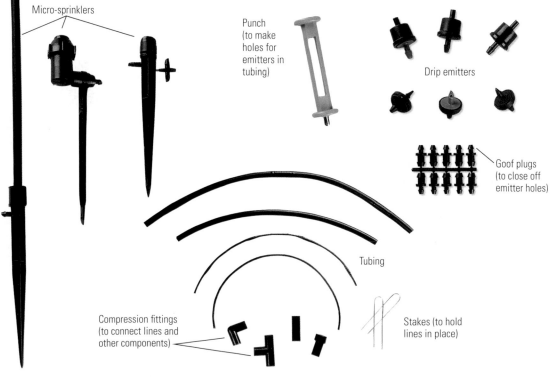

Punch (to make holes for emitters in tubing)

Drip emitters

Goof plugs (to close off emitter holes)

Tubing

Compression fittings (to connect lines and other components)

Stakes (to hold lines in place)

CONNECTING TO YOUR HOUSE WATER SUPPLY

A small drip system can be screwed directly onto an outdoor faucet, but for a multicircuit drip or sprinkler system, you'll have to tap into your water pipes. When doing so, install a shutoff valve so that you can turn off water to the irrigation system without interrupting flow to the house. From the shutoff valve, run pipe to the control valves you'll be putting in for your irrigation system.

Remember to shut off the main water supply first, before the point of connection. If you're apprehensive about tapping into your water pipes, leave this aspect of the job to a professional. Shown at right are connections to an outside faucet (top), an outdoor service line (middle), and a basement meter (bottom).

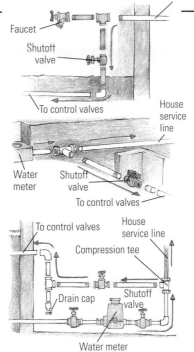

House service line
Faucet
Shutoff valve
To control valves
House service line
Water meter
Shutoff valve
To control valves
To control valves
House service line
Compression tee
Drain cap
Shutoff valve
Water meter

UNDERGROUND DRIP

There is another option for watering turf grass or a meadow, which seems to combine the best features of drip and overhead irrigation: a below-surface low-volume irrigation system. A lattice of specially designed plastic tubing, with embedded emitters, can be buried up to 12 inches below the surface. Water is delivered directly to the grasses' roots, similarly to the way a traditional aboveground drip system works. Although this kind of irrigation is buried like an underground sprinkler system, there are no sprinkler heads that pop up. Underground drip irrigation costs a bit more, but if it's installed correctly, it will provide years and years of efficient and cost-effective watering. Of course this type of line, like any other plastic product in the ground, is susceptible to gopher damage, but it can't be disturbed by foot traffic and can be out of the way of lawn-aeration probes if it's at least 8 inches down.

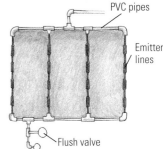

PVC pipes
Emitter lines
Flush valve

OVERHEAD SPRINKLERS

Large plantings of ornamental grasses or meadows can be conveniently irrigated with an overhead watering system, similar to those traditionally used for lawns. Many gardeners like to use overhead irrigation because it simulates natural rainfall, and the evidence of water going to their plants is visible. The choice of sprinklers ranges from a variety of separate movable sprinkler heads attached to a hose, to a permanent underground system of PVC pipe and stationary retractable above-ground sprinklers controlled by a timer.

The amount of time you want to spend watering your grasses will dictate which system you use. It takes no time at all to attach a sprinkler to a hose and water your grass garden in a couple of locations. This kind of water distribution seems to be the only one immune to disturbance by gophers and other animals, assuming that you put away the hose and sprinkler after each use. But if you want to spend less time moving a sprinkler around and irrigate even when you're not there, put in underground irrigation. Planning and installation will take some time in the beginning, but after that the system does the work. However, don't forget to walk around every now and then to make sure the sprinklers are reaching their intended plants.

The biggest disadvantage to overhead watering is the inevitable runoff and waste of water. Some of it trickles away and is not absorbed by the soil, and some evaporates and never makes it to the ground at all. However, certain grasses and grasslike plants benefit from additional water vapor. Some even benefit from the cleansing action of water running down leaves and flowers, but water can weigh down and bend grass stems and flowers. And too much water on the foliage of plants can cause a disease known as rust (see pages 120–121).

Sprinkler heads come in a variety of configurations to target specific areas of your grass and other plantings.

CARING FOR GRASSES

FERTILIZING

All green plants need a certain amount of nutrients in their soil for healthy growth. The nutrients can occur naturally, but sometimes one or more of the three major ones—nitrogen (N), phosphorus (P), and potassium (K)—is lacking. Fertilizers containing the three elements have been developed over the years, some from chemical sources and some—organic fertilizers—derived from naturally occurring materials. Different kinds of fertilizers have various amounts of each element, which are listed on the label as N-P-K with a numerical value for each.

Gardeners usually have strong opinions about the use and misuse of fertilizer, especially chemical fertilizer. Some grass gardeners use no fertilizer at all because they believe it can make the plants grow too quickly and become susceptible to pests and floppy growth. Too much nitrogen not only will weaken certain grass plants, but can work in the opposite extreme and cause aggressive growth in running grasses to the point of invasiveness. And some species of ornamental grasses do best in poor soil.

Other grass gardeners use organic fertilizers with great results. Some feed their grasses or grasslike plants as they do any other perennial; others use fertilizer at one-quarter strength. You will have to determine what fertilizing regimen works best for the grasses in your garden. Please note that it is a common mistake to fertilize a plant that isn't doing well, when there might actually be a pest or disease preying on it, or it may be receiving an incorrect amount of water. An exception to any rule about fertilizing is that grasses in containers will benefit from regular applications of additional nutrients (see page 104).

There isn't a specific nutrient formula you can sprinkle on ornamental grasses to make them look good all the time, but most grass gardeners would agree on the benefits of amending the soil with manure or other organic matter once a year. And don't forget to renew the organic mulch around the plants as it breaks down. Fresh mulch provides a small but steady source of nutrients for your grass and grasslike plants.

Fertilizer types, clockwise from left: soluble crystals (dry and dissolved), dry granules, organic fish meal, timed-release pellets.

Mulching and amending soil is the best possible thing you can do for your garden. Whether a particular material is a mulch or an amendment depends simply on its application; mulch sits on top of the ground, amendments are typically dug into it. Even many grasses, which do not like a rich soil, gain extra benefits from the organic matter, moisture retention, and improved texture provided by these materials. Shown from left to right are organic compost (two types), shredded bark mulch, redwood mulch, forest bark mulch, and peat moss.

GROOMING

Not only do perennial ornamental grasses generally look better if they are cut back once a year, but they are healthier for it. When old growth is cut off, new growth is exposed to healthful air and sunlight. It's a natural part of the life of a grass.

Even prairie grasses have been trimmed and shaped by seasonal fires and grazing cattle or bison for countless centuries. If you don't have grazing animals or are reluctant to burn off the grasses in your yard, a few cutting tools that you probably already have in your garage will do the trick.

Depending on the size and texture of the grasses you are grooming, you can use hand pruners, hedge shears (handheld or electric), or a bow saw to cut off old foliage. Be sure to wear gloves when doing this, as some grass edges are very sharp.

There is no set time of year to trim the old growth from your ornamental grasses. Many grass gardeners like to trim back at the end of winter as new shoots appear. They have discovered the pleasure of leaving the old stalks standing through winter. The stalks give the usually gray, dead-looking garden a point of interest and can be lovely with a dusting of snow. Whenever you decide to trim back your grasses, be sure not to trim them too closely. Some do well with just a general shaping, and some can be cut fairly short. But it's a good idea to trim them to no lower than 4 inches from the ground.

Rows of trimmed *Nassella tenuissima* in a nursery will not retain their shorn appearance for long. Most grasses quickly respond to such pruning with rapid new growth.

Some grasses and grasslike plants can be prickly or irritating. If you need to do some serious pruning, consider a pair of "Armadillos," sleeves made of heavy-duty canvas over duck canvas (see "Sources").

Large sweeps of ornamental grass can be mowed with a lawn mower or cut back with a string trimmer. Such treatment actually improves their growth.

DIVIDING

1 Divide grasses when the clumps become overgrown or the centers die out. When plants are dormant, dig them up by slicing around the root ball with a sharp spade.

2 Pull out the clump and use the spade to slice the crown and root ball into sections. If clumps are very overgrown, you may need to use a saw or sharp knife.

3 Cut back the tops of the clumps and tease apart the roots with your fingers. Replant the divisions in nursery containers or in an amended planting hole.

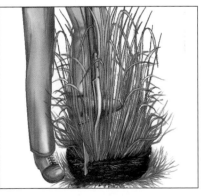

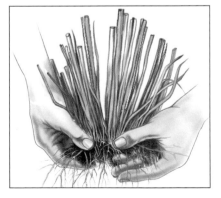

TROUBLESHOOTING

RUST

Rust is a fungal disease that attacks ornamental grasses. It looks like patches of rusty orange spots on the leaves. You can sometimes eradicate it by removing and destroying the infected plant parts. It seems to be most prevalent during humid weather and is less likely to appear when grasses are well spaced so there is plenty of air circulation between them. You can treat rust with wettable sulfur or a fungicide labeled for this use.

Rust

POCKET GOPHERS

This is probably the most common and most unpredictable pest in the western garden. One gopher can shear off a row of grasses at ground level in one night. Gophers do this by chewing the succulent crown of each plant. The best defense against this creature is to surround the root ball of each grass plant with a ½-inch chicken-wire cage before putting the plant into the ground. Alternative methods of control include traps, poisons, and a household cat (though not at the same time!).

MEALYBUGS

Miscanthus species can become infested with mealybugs—very slow-moving insects that are usually introduced to the garden through infected plant material. Inspect new plants for telltale white cottony insects—especially between the stalk and the leaf sheath. You can sometimes eliminate mealybugs by daubing them with alcohol-soaked cotton swabs. But if the infestation is too great, you may need to throw away or burn the plant (do not put infested plants into the compost pile).

Mites and webbing

MITES

The only ornamental grass that seems to be affected by mites is bamboo. And the best defense against mites is to avoid bringing them into your garden in the first place. Inspect new bamboo plants thoroughly. Look for small bleached-looking spots and tiny white webs on the undersides of leaves; if you see these, you may be able to remove the mites at this point by thoroughly spraying the plants with water through a high-powered nozzle.

CROWN ROT

The crown of a grass plant is where the roots join the stem. If the crown is covered with soil or mulch that is kept continuously damp, it can simply rot away and the plant will die. The best way to avoid this problem is to plant correctly. Plant each grass at the same soil level it was in the nursery container, make sure the soil drains well, and don't pile mulch too closely to the plant stems.

SLUGS

Most ornamental grasses are not susceptible to damage from slugs—with the exception of sedges and grasses with soft or succulent leaves. There is really no way to completely eradicate these pests, but a few remedies can help keep them under control. Pick off the slugs at night by hand, or put strips of copper around the grasses they like. Leave out traps made of shallow cups of flat beer, or maintain a dry sprinkling of diatomaceous earth on the soil. Nontoxic and toxic baits are also available at garden centers.

FLOPPY GROWTH

A grass or grasslike plant can have floppy growth when the plant grows too quickly—usually as a result of too much nitrogen or fertilizer—or if it is not receiving enough light. Stems are uncharacteristically thin and can't hold up their flowers. To keep them upright, large grasses can be staked to metal pipes in or near the plant's base. Narrower stakes can be inserted as the grass gets stronger. Smaller floppy-stemmed grasses can be secured with coated wire stakes found at nurseries or garden centers. Homemade bamboo stakes or tepees blend especially well with grasses (see page 111).

FIRE

In the West there is always concern about wildfires during the summer months. Dry, ungroomed ornamental grasses make perfect tinder for such a fire. If you live in a fire-prone area, you should be very careful with large grass plantings or meadows. Keep them 30 feet or more away from your house. Cut back plants to 4 inches from the ground as soon as the foliage ripens. Any plant will burn if it gets hot enough, but a few particular grasses should be avoided in fire-prone areas: any cool-season (summer-dormant) grasses such as *Stipa* or *Muhlenbergia,* and all *Pennisetum* species. For more information on fire-safe plantings, contact your local Cooperative Extension Office.

Controlled burn

INVASIVENESS

The invasive potential of grasses and grasslike plants is often a concern with gardeners. Even seasoned veterans exercise caution when new grasses are introduced and their invasive potential may not have been evaluated in all climates. But most ornamental grasses grow in clumps and are not invasive. And what is invasive in one region may not be a problem in another. If you are interested in planting a grass (like bamboo) that reproduces with rhizomes, look into barriers or containment products that will keep the plant in one area (see page 115). Don't plant grasses with unknown invasive potential near an open field. Never collect grasses in the wild. Even if they look contained in the environment where you found them, they could behave differently in your garden. Check with a local horticultural society or your local Cooperative Extension Office to learn about known invasive grasses in your area.

WEEDS

Weeds in your ornamental grass garden compete for the same soil and water as more desirable plants. So it's a good idea to be diligent about pulling them out, but this can be a challenge if the emerging weeds resemble the grasses you have planted. Until you become familiar with the weeds in your garden, mark your desirable grasses with tags or labels. When establishing a new meadow or natural lawn planting, you'll find weed control to be the major task for the first few seasons. Be patient; eventually the desirable grasses will crowd out the weeds. Meanwhile, mulch heavily and pull weeds by hand or use a degradable product such as glyphosate to spot-control stubborn weeds.

Weeds or flowers?

ALLERGIES

Every year more and more people seem to complain of having allergy symptoms when they go outside. Grass pollens may be contributing to seasonal sneezing and itchy eyes, but no more so than many other pollen-producing plants. But if you do suffer from allergies, there are a few things you can do keep yourself sneeze-free. First, be sure to plant a variety of grasses in your garden. Second, request female grasses from the nursery, if possible, as only male plants produce pollen. Third, mow regularly to keep grasses from producing flowers, and wear a mask when mowing or trimming. Finally, if allergies are truly a problem for you or your family, avoid the following grasses, which are strongly allergenic: *Anthoxanthum,* all brome grasses except cheat *(Bromus secalinus),* nonhybrid Bermuda grass, *Dactylis,* and tender fountain grass *(Pennisetum setaceum).*

GRASSES AND GRASSLIKE PLANTS

Hardiness and climate adaptability is not known for all grasses. If in doubt about the suitability of a plant for your area, check with a knowledgeable local source.

GENUS	SPECIES AND COMMON NAME(S)	COMMENTS
Achnatherum	calamagrostis SILVER SPIKE GRASS; A. hymenoides INDIAN RICE GRASS; A. speciosum DESERT NEEDLE GRASS	Clumping, cool-season growers. A. calamagrostis may be hardy to −25°F; others are frost-tender. A. hymenoides syn. Oryzopsis hymenoides.
Acorus	calamus SWEET FLAG, variegated form 'Variegatus'; A. gramineus JAPANESE SWEET FLAG, variegated form 'Variegatus', dwarf form 'Pusillus'	Clumping, low-growing perennial. Leaves scented when crushed. Generally hardy to −5°F; A calamus to −25°F. Needs plentiful water; give some shade in hottest areas.
Agrostis	canina 'Silver Needles'; A. gigantea REDTOP; A. pallens BENT GRASS; A. scabra TICKLE GRASS; A. stolonifera CREEPING BENT	A. canina and A. stolonifera are evergreen. Hardy to −35°F.
Alopecurus	pratensis MEADOW FOXTAIL, variegated form 'Variegatus'	Cool-season grower that spreads slowly by rhizomes. Hardy to −25°F.
Ammophila	breviligulata AMERICAN BEACH GRASS	Warm-season coastal grass; European species A. arenaria invasive in some areas. Hardy to −15°F.
Andropogon	gerardii BIG BLUESTEM; A. saccharoides SILVER BEARD GRASS; A. ternarius SPLIT-BEARD BROOM SEDGE; A. virginicus BROOM SEDGE	Clumping, warm-season grasses, many native to North America. Hardy to −5°F; A. gerardii to −25°F.
Anthoxanthum	odoratum SWEET VERNAL GRASS	Clumping, cool-season grower. Leaves fragrant when crushed. Hardy to −15°F.
Aristida	purpurea PURPLE THREE-AWN	Clumping grass native to dry areas of North America. May self-sow. Hardy to −5°F.
Arrhenatherum	elatius bulbosum BULBOUS OAT GRASS, variegated form 'Variegatum' STRIPED BULBOUS OAT GRASS	Clumping, cool-season grower. Needs shade in hottest areas. Species may be invasive. Hardy to −25°F.
Arundo	donax GIANT REED; A. formosana TAIWAN GRASS	Tall, bamboolike grower to 20 ft. May be invasive in moist, warm areas. Hardy to −5°F.
Askidiosperma	paniculatum	Clumping, reedlike restio.
Astelia	nervosa chathamica SILVER SPEAR	Perennial with straplike leaves. Needs some shade. Frost-tender.
Baumea	rubiginosa	Aquatic plant; hardy to 5°F.
Bouteloua	curtipendula SIDE-OATS GRAMA; B. gracilis BLUE GRAMA, MOSQUITO GRASS	Clumping, warm-season growers native to short-grass prairie. Hardy to −25°F. Can be used as lawn.
Briza	maxima RATTLESNAKE GRASS, QUAKING GRASS; annual species B. media	Clumping, cool-season grower with distinctive flower heads. Hardy to −25°F.
Bromus	inermis GOLDEN BROME GRASS; B. i. 'Skinner's Gold' SMOOTH BROME; B. kalmii PRAIRIE BROME	Perennial naturalized in North America. Spreads by rhizomes. Hardy to 5°F.
Buchloe	dactyloides BUFFALO GRASS	Warm-season grower; spreads by stolons. Can be used as lawn. Drought tolerant. Hardy to −25°F.
Calamagrostis	× acutiflora FEATHER REED GRASS; C. × a. 'Karl Foerster' KARL FOERSTER FEATHER REED GRASS, C. × a. 'Overdam' VARIEGATED FEATHER REED GRASS; C. foliosa MENDOCINO REED GRASS; C. nutkaensis PACIFIC REED GRASS	Clumping, upright, cool-season growers. Highly ornamental. Most species do not like hot, humid conditions. Hardiness varies; C. × acutiflora to −25°F; C. foliosa and C. nutkaensis frost-tender.
Carex	baccans CRIMSON-SEEDED SEDGE; C. bergrenii NEW ZEALAND SEDGE; C. buchananii LEATHER LEAF SEDGE; C. caryophyllea 'The Beatles' MOP-HEADED SEDGE; C. comans NEW ZEALAND HAIR SEDGE; C. dolichostachya 'Kaga Nishiki' (Gold Fountains); C. elata TUFTED SEDGE; C.e. 'Aurea' ('Bowles Golden'); firma 'Variegata'; C. flacca (glauca) BLUE SEDGE; C. flagellifera; C. fraseriana FRASER'S SEDGE; C. 'Frosted Curls'; C. grayi GRAY'S SEDGE; C. morrowii JAPANESE SEDGE, C. m. temnolepis HOSOBA KAN SUGE, variegated form C. m. expallida 'Variegata'; C. muskingumensis PALM SEDGE, forms include 'Oehme', 'Silberstreif', 'Wachtposten'; C. nigra BLACK-FLOWERING SEDGE; C. nudata CALIFORNIA BLACK-FLOWERING SEDGE; C. oshimensis 'Evergold' ('Aureo-variegata', 'Old Gold'); C. pansa CALIFORNIA MEADOW SEDGE	Clumping or rhizomatous growers, mostly shade- and moisture-loving but some tolerate wide range of conditions. Lowest types used as lawns. Some sedges are evergreen in mild climates; hardiness varies by species.

GENUS	SPECIES AND COMMON NAMES	COMMENTS
Carex	pendula GREAT DROOPING SEDGE; C. pensylvanica PENNSYLVANIA SEDGE, C. perdentata TEXAS MEADOW SEDGE; C. senta BALTIMORE SEDGE; C. siderosticha 'Variegata' STRIPED BROAD-LEAFED SEDGE; C. solandri; C. spissa SAN DIEGO SEDGE; C. sylvatica FOREST SEDGE; C. testacea ORANGE NEW ZEALAND SEDGE; C. texensis CATLIN SEDGE; C. tumulicola BERKELEY SEDGE	See previous entry.
Chasmanthium	latifolium WILD OATS	Clumping, warm-season grower with distinctive flower heads. Easy to grow; may self-sow. Hardy to −15°F.
Chionochloa	rubra SNOW GRASS, RED TUSSOCK GRASS	Clumping New Zealand native. Frost-tender.
Chloris	virgata FINGER GRASS	Clumping, subtropical spreader. Frost-tender.
Chondropetalum	tectorum CAPE RUSH	Rushlike, cool-season restio. Frost-tender.
Coix	lacryma-jobi JOB'S TEARS	Annual grower with unusual beadlike seed heads.
Cortaderia	selloana PAMPAS GRASS, forms include 'Albolineata' ('Silver Stripe'), 'Andes Silver', 'Aureolineata', 'Bertini', 'Monstrosa', 'Monvin' (Sun Stripe), 'Patagonia', 'Pink Feather', 'Pumila' COMPACT PAMPAS GRASS, 'Rosea', 'Silver Comet'; C. jubata PURPLE PAMPAS GRASS; C. richardii TUSSOCK GRASS	Tall, clumping, warm-season growers. C. jubata invasive in California. C. selloana evergreen in warm climates. Frost-tender.
Cymbopogon	citratus LEMON GRASS	Clumping, strongly lemon-scented; used for culinary purposes. Frost-tender.
Cyperus	alternifolius UMBRELLA PLANT; C. eragrostis PALE GALINGALE; C. giganteus GIANT PAPYRUS; C. papyrus PAPYRUS; C. prolifer DWARF PAPYRUS; C. testacea SLENDER PAPYRUS	Tropical, semiaquatic plants. Frost-tender.
Dactylis	glomerata 'Variegata' VARIEGATED ORCHARD GRASS	Clumping, cool-season grower. Hardy to −15°F.
Danthonia	californica CALIFORNIA OAT GRASS; D. spicata POVERTY OAT GRASS	Hardy to −25°F.
Deschampsia	cespitosa TUFTED HAIR GRASS; forms include D.c. 'Bronze-schleier', 'Fairy's Joke', 'Goldgehaenge', 'Goldschleier', 'Gold-staub', 'Goldtau', 'Northern Lights', ' Schottland', 'Tardiflora', 'Tautraeger', D. c. beringensis TUFTED HAIR GRASS, D. c. holci-formis PACIFIC HAIR GRASS; D. flexuosa CRINKLED HAIR GRASS	Clumping, cool-season growers. Dramatic flower heads. Some hardy to −25°F or colder.
Elegia	capensis BROOM REED	Tall, clumping, rushlike restio. Frost-tender.
Eleocharis	dulcis CHINESE WATER CHESTNUT; E. palustris	Semiaquatic Asian native; spreads by stolons. Edible tubers. Frost-tender.
Elymus	canadensis CANADA WILD RYE; E. condensatus; E. hispidus WILD RYE, LYME GRASS; E. magellanicus MAGELLAN WHEATGRASS, BLUE WHEATGRASS; E. virginicus VIRGINIA WILD RYE	Clumping perennials. E. magellanicus is cool-season grower with intensely blue foliage; hardy to −5°F. E. canadensis is prairie grass; may self-sow; hardy to −35°F.
Equisetum	contorta MINIATURE CONTORTED HORSETAIL; E. hyemale HORSETAIL; E. scirpoides DWARF HORSETAIL	Rushlike, semiaquatic plants. Can be extremely invasive.
Eragrostis	curvula WEEPING LOVE GRASS, AFRICAN LOVE GRASS; E. elliotii BLUE LOVE GRASS; refracta FIELD LOVE GRASS; E. spectabilis PURPLE LOVE GRASS, TUMBLE GRASS; E. trichodes SAND LOVE GRASS	Clumping, warm-season growers. May self-sow. E. curvula and E. contortus hardy to 5°F; E. spectabilis and E. contortus hardy to −15°F.
Erianthus	contortus BENT-AWN PLUME GRASS	Clumping, warm-season grower. Hardy to −5°F.
Eriophorum	angustifolium COTTON GRASS	Bog native. Needs cool summers. Hardy to −35°F.
Festuca	amethystina LARGE BLUE FESCUE, forms include 'April Green', 'Superba', 'Klose', 'Bronzeglanz'; F. californica CALIFORNIA FESCUE; F. filiformis HAIR FESCUE; F. gigantea GIANT FESCUE; F. glauca (F. ovina, F. cinerea) BLUE FESCUE, forms include 'Azurit', 'Blaufink', 'Blausilber', 'Elijah Blue', 'Meerblau', 'Solling'; F. mairei ATLAS FESCUE; F. rubra RED FESCUE	Fine-textured, mostly clumping, cool-season growers. Most prefer full sun and need good drainage. F. glauca used as ground cover plant. F. rubra used as lawn. Most hardy to −15°F or −25°F.
Glyceria	maxima MANNA GRASS, variegated form 'Variegata'	Bog plant that spreads by rhizomes. Hardy to −15°F; not for hot regions.
Hakonechloa	macra JAPANESE FOREST GRASS, HAKONE GRASS, variegated forms 'Albovariegata', 'All Gold', 'Aureola'	Spreads slowly by rhizomes; prefers moist conditions. Hardy to −15°F.

GENUS	SPECIES AND COMMON NAMES	COMMENTS
Helictotrichon	sempervirens BLUE OAT GRASS, BLUE AVENA GRASS	Clumping, cool-season grower. Needs good drainage. Hardy to −25°F.
Hierochloe	occidentalis CALIFORNIA SWEET GRASS; H. odorata VANILLA GRASS, HOLY GRASS	Spreads by rhizomes; prefers moist conditions. Fragrant foliage. H. occidentalis hardy to 5°F; H. odorata to −25°F.
Holcus	mollis CREEPING SOFT GRASS, variegated form 'Variegatus' ('Albovariegatus')	Cool-season grower that spreads by rhizomes. Hardy to −15°F.
Hordeum	jubatum FOXTAIL BARLEY	Clumping, cool-season grower. Self-sows; may be invasive. Hardy to −25°F.
Hystrix	patula BOTTLEBRUSH GRASS	Clumping, cool-season grower. Tolerates dry shade. Hardy to −25°F.
Imperata	cylindrica 'Rubra' ('Red Baron') JAPANESE BLOOD GRASS	Spreads by rhizomes; species only is invasive. Striking red foliage. Hardy to −5°F.
Juncus	effusus SOFT RUSH, COMMON RUSH, striped form 'Gold Strike', J. e. 'Spiralis' CORKSCREW RUSH; J. inflexus HARD RUSH; J. patens; J. p. 'Carmen's Gray' CALIFORNIA GRAY RUSH	Moisture-loving perennials. Hardiness varies from 5°F (J. patens) to −25°F (J. effusus).
Koeleria	glauca BLUE HAIR GRASS; K. macrantha HAIR GRASS, JUNE GRASS	Clumping, cool-season growers. K. glauca hardy to −5°F. K. macrantha can be used for natural lawns; hardy to −25°.
Lagurus	ovatus HARE'S TAIL GRASS	Annual grower. Fluffy, egg-shaped flower heads.
Leymus	arenarius BLUE LYME GRASS; L. condensatus GIANT WILD RYE; L. c. 'Canyon Prince'; L. mollis SEA LYME GRASS; L. racemosus GIANT BLUE RYE; L. triticoides 'Grey Dawn'	Cool-season grower; spreads by rhizomes but not usually aggressive. L. condensatus native to California; hardy to 5°F. Others hardy to −25°F.
Liriope	muscari BIG BLUE LILY TURF, variegated form 'Variegata'. Closely related to Ophiopogon	Shade-loving low grower; used as ground cover, especially in South. Hardy to −5°F.
Luzula	luzuloides WOODRUSH; L. nivea SNOWY WOODRUSH; L. pilosa HAIRY WOODRUSH; L. purpurea PURPLE WOODRUSH; L. sylvatica GREATER WOODRUSH	Shade-loving, clumping or spread by rhizomes. Species and cvs. vary from −5°F to −25°F.
Melica	altissima, M. a. 'Alba', M. a. 'Atropurpurea' SIBERIAN MELIC; M. ciliata HAIRY MELIC GRASS; M. imperfecta COAST RANGE MELIC	Clumping, cool-season growers. M. altissima and M. ciliata hardy to −15°F, possibly more. M. imperfecta frost-tender.
Milium	effusum 'Aureum' GOLDEN WOOD MILLET, BOWLES' GOLDEN GRASS	Clumping, cool-season grower for shady, moist conditions. Hardy to −5°F.
Miscanthus	floridulus GIANT MISCANTHUS; M. 'Giganteus' GIANT SILVER GRASS; M. sacchariflorus SILVER BANNER GRASS; M. sinensis MAIDEN GRASS, EULALIA; forms include 'Adagio', 'Aethiopien', 'Arabesque', 'Autumn Light', 'Blondo', 'Condensatus' PURPLE BLOOMING JAPANESE SILVER GRASS, 'Dixieland', 'Ferner Osten', 'Flamingo', 'Goldfeder' 'Goliath', 'Gracillimus', MAIDEN GRASS, 'Graziella', 'Hinjo' (Little Nicky), 'Kascade', 'Kirk Alexander', 'Little Kitten' 'Malepartus', 'Morning Light', 'Mt. Washington', 'Nippon', 'November Sunset', 'Purpurascens' FLAME GRASS, 'Sarabande', 'Silberfeder', 'Silberpfeil', 'Strictus' PORCUPINE GRASS, 'Undine' 'Variegatus' VARIEGATED MISCANTHUS, 'Yaku Jima', 'Zebrinus' ZEBRA GRASS; M.s. condensatus 'CABARET', 'COSMOPOLITAN'; M. transmorrisonensis EVERGREEN MISCANTHUS	Graceful, clumping, warm-season growers with showy full flowerheads. Best with plentiful moisture. May naturalize in optimal conditions. Hardiness varies; most hardy to −15°F. Numerous cvs. available.
Molinia	caerulea MOOR GRASS, forms include 'Heidebraut', 'Moor-flamme', 'Moorhexe', 'Strahlenquelle', 'Variegata'; M. c. arun-dinacea TALL PURPLE MOOR GRASS, forms include 'Karl Foerster', 'Skyracer', 'Transparent', 'Windspiel'	Clumping, cool-season growers that prefer moist, cool con-ditions. Hardy to −15°F.
Muhlenbergia	capillaris PINK MUHLY; M. dumosa BAMBOO MUHLY; M. filipes GULF MUHLY; M. lindheimeri LINDHEIMER'S MUHLY; M. rigens DEER GRASS; M. rigida PURPLE MUHLY; M. wrightii SPIKE MUHLY	Mostly clumping, warm-season growers, native to southern United States and Mexico. Most drought-tolerant, sun lovers. None hardy below −5°F; most are frost-tender.
Nassella	pulchra PURPLE NEEDLE GRASS; N. tenuissima MEXICAN FEATHER GRASS	Showy, cool-season growers with fine texture. N. tenuissima syn. Stipa tenuissima; may self sow. Hardy to −5°F.
Nolinia	microcarpa BEAR GRASS	Prized for arrangements. Hardy to 5°F.
Ophiopogon	japonicus MONDO GRASS, dwarf form 'Kyoto Dwarf'; O. planis-capus 'Nigrescens'. Closely related to Liriope.	Low-growing, spreading grasslike ground cover plant. Frost-tender.
Panicum	virgatum SWITCH GRASS, PANIC GRASS; forms include 'Blue Tower', 'Cloud Nine', 'Dallas Blues', 'Haense Herms', 'Heavy Metal', 'Prairie Sky', 'Shenandoah', 'Strictum', 'Trailblazer', 'Warrior'	Clumping or rhizomatous growers. Prairie native; warm-season grass. May be prone to rust. Hardy to −25°F.

GENUS	SPECIES AND COMMON NAMES	COMMENTS
Pennisetum	alopecuroides FOUNTAIN GRASS, forms include 'Cassian', 'Cauda-tum' WHITE-FLOWERING FOUNTAIN GRASS, 'Moudry' BLACK-FLOWERING FOUNTAIN GRASS, 'Little Bunny', 'Little Honey', 'National Arbore-tum', 'Paul's Giant', 'Woodside', dwarf form 'Hameln'; P. 'Burgundy Giant'; P. flaccidum; P. messaicum; P. orientale; P. setaceum TENDER FOUNTAIN GRASS, forms include 'Eaton Canyon' COMPACT PURPLE FOUNTAIN GRASS, 'Rubrum' (syn. 'Cupreum', 'Atropurpureum'); P. villosum FEATHERTOP; P. viridescens	Varied and showy, mostly clumping, warm-season growers. Tender types may be grown as annuals. P. setaceum and P. villosum may be invasive in mild climates.
Phalaris	arundinacea RIBBON GRASS, REED CANARY GRASS, forms include 'Feesey' ('Strawberries and Cream'), 'Luteopicta', 'Picta', ('Ele-gantissima') GARDENER'S GARTERS, 'Tricolor', 'Woods Dwarf'	Cool-season grower; can spread invasively by rhizomes in moist conditions. Many forms highly variegated. Hardy to −25°F; needs shade in hottest climates.
Phormium	cookianum MOUNTAIN FLAX; P. tenax NEW ZEALAND FLAX, many forms	Evergreen New Zealand native. Easy to grow; frost-tender.
Phragmites	australis COMMON REED, variegated form P. a. aurea ('Variegatus')	Warm-season, moisture-loving grower. Spreads by rhizomes. Hardy to −25°F.
Poa	arachnifera TEXAS BLUEGRASS	Clumping, cool-season grower. Related to bluegrasses used as turf. Hardy to −5°F.
Restio	festucaeformis; R. quadratus; R. tetraphyllum	Cool-season, rushlike plants native to South Africa and Aus-tralia.
Rhynchelytrum	repens RUBY GRASS; R. nerviglume NATAL RUBY GRASS	Clumping, cool-season grass. Striking flowers. Frost-tender.
Saccharum	arundinaceum HARDY SUGAR CANE; S. officinarum SUGAR CANE; S. ravennae RAVENNA GRASS	Tall, clumping warm-season growers. Source of sugar; more ornamental forms under development. Frost-tender. S. ravennae hardy to −5°F.
Schizachyrium	scoparium LITTLE BLUESTEM, PRAIRIE BEARD GRASS, forms include 'Aldous', 'Little Camper', 'Blaze', 'The Blues'	Clumping, warm-season grower; native to tall-grass prairie. Hardy to −35°F.
Schoenoplectus	subterminalis SWAYING RUSH; S. tabernaemontani GREAT BULRUSH; S. t. 'Zebrinus' ZEBRA BULRUSH	Aquatic, warm-season growers. Some may be hardy to −15°F.
Scirpus	cernuus (syn. Isolepis cernua) FIBER-OPTICS PLANT	Moisture-loving, frost-tender plant.
Sesleria	autumnalis AUTUMN MOOR GRASS; S. caerulea BLUE MOOR GRASS; S. heufleriana BLUE-GREEN MOOR GRASS; S. nitida GRAY MOOR GRASS	Clumping, cool-season growers. Tolerate most conditions, including alkaline soil. Many used as evergreen ground cover. Hardy to −25°F.
Setaria	palmifolia PALM GRASS	Wide-leafed, clumping, warm-season grower. Frost-tender.
Sorghastrum	nutans INDIAN GRASS, forms include 'Holt', 'Osage', 'Rumsey', 'Sioux Blue'	Clumping, warm-season grower; native to tall-grass prairie. Tolerates many conditions. Hardy to −25°F.
Spartina	patens MARSH HAY, SALT HAY; S. pectinata PRAIRIE CORD GRASS; variegated form 'Aureomarginata' ('Variegata')	Warm-season grower; spreads by rhizomes. Native to salt-water or freshwater habitats. Hardy to −25°F.
Spodiopogon	sibericus SIBERIAN GRAYBEARD	Clumping, warm-season grower. Needs moisture, some shade. Hardy to −25°F.
Sporobolus	airoides ALKALI DROPSEED, ALKALI SACATON; S. heterolepis PRAIRIE DROPSEED; S. wrightii GIANT SACATON	Clumping, warm-season growers; prairie natives. S. airoides hardy to −15°F; S. heterolepis to −25°F.
Stipa	arundinacea FEATHER GRASS; S. barbata; S. capillata; S. gigantea GIANT FEATHER GRASS; S. lepida FOOTHILL FEATHER GRASS; S. pulchra PURPLE NEEDLE GRASS; S. ramosissima PILLAR OF SMOKE	Clumping, cool-season growers. Most prefer sunny, open conditions. Mostly frost-tender; S. capillata hardy to 5°F.
Themeda	japonica (T. triandra japonica) JAPANESE THEMEDA	Clumping, warm-season grower. May be hardy to −25°F.
Tridens	flavus PURPLETOP	Clumping, warm-season grower; native to East Coast. Hardy to −25°F. May self-sow.
Tripsacum	dactyloides EASTERN GAMA GRASS	Spreads by rhizomes; prefers moist sites. Hardy to −15°F.
Typha	angustifolia NARROW-LEAFED CATTAIL; T. latifolia COMMON CATTAIL; T. minima MINIATURE CATTAIL	Moisture-loving plants that spread by rhizomes. Larger types can be invasive. Some hardy to −35°F.
Uncinia	egmontiana ORANGE HOOK SEDGE; U. rubra RED HOOK SEDGE	Clumping sedges native to New Zealand; require cool, moist growing conditions; frost-tender.
Uniola	paniculata SEA OATS	Warm-season grower; spreads by rhizomes. Native to east-ern United States; used for dune stabilization. Hardy to 5°F.
Vetiveria	zizanioides VETIVER, KHUS KHUS	Clumping, warm-season grower; source of fragrant oil. Frost-tender. Evergreen in mild climates.

SOURCES

WHOLESALE NURSERIES

KURT BLUEMEL INC.
2740 Greene Lane
Baldwin, MD 21013
800/248-7584
Fax 410/557-9785
www.bluemel.com
Wholesale and retail grower and supplier of ornamental grasses, bamboo, sedges, rushes, ferns, and perennials.

GREENLEE NURSERY
241 E. Franklin Avenue
Pomona, CA 91766
909/629-9045
Fax 909/620-9283
grnleenrsn@aol.com
Carry largest selection of ornamental grasses on the west coast. Fax or e-mail requests for availability and pricing.

SAN MARCOS GROWERS
125 South San Marcos Road
Santa Barbara, CA 93111
805/683-1561
Fax 805/964-1329
www.smgrowers.com
Specialize in grasses appropriate for California gardens.

MAIL ORDER PLANTS

AMBER WAVES GARDENS
1460 Hillandale Road
Benton Harbor, MI 49022
AmberWaveG@aol.com
www.amberwavegardens.com
Grower of hostas, hardy bamboo, and ornamental grasses.

APPALACHIAN WILDFLOWER NURSERY
723 Honey Creek Road
Reedsville, PA 17084
717/667-6998
donhackenberry@lcworkshop.com
Specialize in native and non-native plants for woodlands and open spaces.

BAMBOO SOURCERY
Sebastopol, CA
707/823-5866
www.bamboo.nu
Specialty nursery with over 300 species of bamboo.

THE BAMBOO GARDEN
Portland, OR
503/654-0024
Fax 503/231-9387
www.bamboogarden.com
Visit by appointment only. Call or e-mail for availability and pricing.

BAMBOO GARDENER
2609 NW 86th Street
Seattle, Washington 98117
206-782-3490
www.bamboogardener.com
bambuguru@earthlink.net
Nursery, mail order bamboo and book business.

BEAVER CREEK
7526 Pelleaux Road
Knoxville, TN 37938
Phone and fax 865/922-3961
Offer a wide variety of ornamental grasses. Call for a catalog, cost $2.

BLUESTEM NURSERY
1946 Fife Road
Christina Lake, BC
Canada V0H 1E3
Phone and fax 250/447-6363
Offer hardy grasses, sedges, and rushes for colder climates. Both native and exotic plants available.

BLUESTONE PERENNIALS INC.
7211 Middle Ridge Road
Madison, OH 44057-3096
Phone and fax 800/852-5243
www.bluestoneperennials.com
Offer over 800 varieties of perennials including several grasses.

DIGGING DOG NURSERY
P. O. Box 471
Albion, CA 95410
707/937-1130
Fax 707/937-2480
www.diggingdog.com
business@diggingdog.com
National mail order nursery specializing in hard to find perennials, ornamental grasses, shrubs, trees and vines.

FOREST FARM
990 Tetherow Road
Williams, OR 97544-9599
541/846-7269
Fax 541/846-6963
www.forestfarm.com
Extensive 500-page plant catalog for $5.00, or view offerings on-line

FREE SPIRIT NURSERY
20405 32nd Avenue
Langley, BC
Canada V2Z 2C7
Fax 604/530-3776
Ornamental grasses, "new wave" perennials and woodland plants. Fax or write for a list, cost is $1.50.

FRESHWATER FARMS INC.
5851 Myrtle Avenue
Eureka, CA 95503-9510
800/200-8969
Fax 707/442-2490
www.freshwaterfarms.com
info@freshwaterfarms.com
Specialize in California native riparian and wetland plants.

GLASSHOUSE WORKS
Church Street
P. O. Box 97
Stewart, OH 45778-0097
800/837-2142
www.glasshouseworks.com
Specialize in traditional and unusual plants and grasses.

HERONSWOOD NURSERY
7530 NE 288th Street
Kingston, WA 98346-9502
360/297-4172
Fax 360/297-8321
www.heronswood.com
heronswood@silverlink.net
Collect, propagate and sell rare and unusual plants.

HIGH COUNTRY GARDENS
2902 Rufina Street
Santa Fe, NM 87505-2929
800/925-9387
www.highcountrygardens.com

HORTICO INC.
723 Robson Road, R. R. #1
Waterdown, Ontario
Canada L0R 2H1
905/689-6984 or 689-3002
Fax 905/689-6566
www.hortico.com
office@hortico.com
Offer over 500 varieties of traditional and new plants including hostas, bamboo, ornamental grasses, ferns, and bog plants.

JOY CREEK NURSERY
20300 NW Watson Road
Scappoose, OR 97056
503/543-7474
Fax 503/543-6933
www.joycreek.com

LILYPONS WATER GARDENS
6800 Lilypons Road
Box 10
Buckeystown, MD 21717-0010
800/999-5459
Fax 800/879-5459
www.lilypons.com
info@lilypons.com
Offer large selection of water lilies, bog plants, hardy reeds, rushes, and water gardening accessories.

LIMEROCK ORNAMENTAL GRASSES
70 Sawmill Road
Port Matilda, PA 16870
814/692-2272
Fax 814/692-9848
www.limerock.com
limerock@juno.com
Grower and supplier of ornamental and native grasses, rushes, sedges and companion perennials.

NICHE GARDENS
1111 Dawson Road
Chapel Hill, NC 27516
919/967-0078
Fax 919/967-4026
www.nichegardens.com
mail@nichegardens.com
Specialize in wildflowers, southeastern natives, ornamental grasses, and perennials.

PLANT DELIGHTS NURSERY INC.
9241 Sauls Road
Raleigh, NC 27603
919/772-4794
Fax 919/662-0370
www.plantdelights.com
office@plantdelights.com
Wide selection of unusual grasses and companion plants.

PRAIRIE MOON NURSERY
Route 3, Box 1633
Winona, MN 55987-9515
507/452-1362
Fax 507/454-5238
www.prairiemoonnursery.com
pmnrsy@luminet.net
Native plants and seed for wetland, prairie, savanna and woodland.

PRAIRIE NURSERY
P. O. Box 306
W5875 Dyke Avenue
Westfield, WI 53964
800/476-9453
Fax 608/296-2741
www.prairienursery.com
cs@prairienursery.com
Grower and supplier of native prairie grasses and wildflowers.

TRADEWINDS BAMBOO NURSERY
28446 Hunter Creek Loop
Gold Beach, OR 97444
Phone and fax 541/247-0835
www.bamboodirect.com
gib@bamboodirect.com
Specialize in growing over 200 varieties of bamboo.

TRIPPLE BROOK FARM
37 Middle Road
Southampton, MA 01073
413/527-4626
Fax 413/527-9853
www.tripplebrookfarm.com
info@tripplebrookfarm.com
Offer over 300 species of plants including eastern natives, hardy bamboos, ornamental grasses, ferns, mosses, perennials and unusual fruits.

VAN NESS WATER GARDENS
2460 North Euclid Avenue
Upland, CA 91784-1199
800/205-2425
Fax 909/949-7217
www.vnwg.com
vnwg@vnwg.com

ANDRE VIETTE
P.O. Box 1109
Long Meadow road
Fisherville, VA 22939
540/943-2315
Fax 540/943-0782
www.viette.com
Daylilies, iris, and other perennials.

MAIL-ORDER SEEDS/PRAIRIE MIXES

DEGIORGI SEED COMPANY
6011 N Street
Omaha, NE 68117-1634
800/858-2580
402/731-3901
Fax 402/731-8475
www.degiorgiseed.com
Specialize in seeds for vegetables, ornamental grasses, annual and perennial flowers, herbs, gourds, and unusual plants.

ION EXCHANGE, NATIVE SEED AND PLANT NURSERY
1878 Old Mission Drive
Harpers Ferry, IA 52146-7533
800/291-2143
Fax 563/535-7362
www.ionxchange.com
hbright@acegroup.cc
Wide selection of Midwestern native plants, seeds and seed mixes including grasses, sedges, rushes and wildflowers.

NATIVE AMERICAN SEED
Mail Order Station 127
127 N. 16th St.
Junction, TX 76849
800/728-4043
www.seedsource.com
Specialize in locating, harvesting and supplying wildflower and grass seeds native to the Southern Plains.

PEACEFUL VALLEY FARM SUPPLY
110 Springhill Drive
P.O. Box 2209
Grass Valley, CA 95945
888/784-1722
Fax 530/272-4794
www.groworganic.com
contact@groworganic.com

PLANTS OF THE SOUTHWEST
3095 Agua Fria Street
Santa Fe, NM 87507
800/788-7333
Fax 505/438-8800
www.plantsofthesouthwest.com
Supplier of seed for native shrubs, trees, grasses and wildflowers.

SEEDS TRUST
4150 B Black Oak Drive
Box 1048
Hailey, ID 83333-1048
208/788-4363
Fax 208/788-3452
www.seedstrust.com
orders@seedsave.org
Specialize in non-hybrid and heirloom vegetable, herb, and native grass and wildflower seeds for high altitude gardens.

WESTERN NATIVE SEED
P. O. Box 188
Coaldale, CO 81222
719/942-3955
Fax 942-3605
www.westernnativeseed.com
westseed@chaffee.net

ORGANIZATIONS

ORNAMENTAL GRASS SOCIETY
P. O. Box 11144
St. Paul, MN 55111-0144
612/729-1573
www.ornamentalgrasssociety.org
mail@ornamentalgrasssociety.org
Fledgling organization dedicated to ornamental grasses.

WILD ONES
P.O. Box 1274
Appleton, WI 54912-1274
920/730-3986
Fax 920/730-8654
www.for-wild.org
woresource@aol.com
Non-profit organization with regional chapters in several states. Mission is to share information about environmentally sound landscaping using native species.

COOPERATIVE EXTENSION OFFICES
To search on the Internet for the nearest Cooperative Extension Office (usually affiliated with a university), type in a search engine the words "Cooperative Extension" and your city, county, or state. To find the phone number, look in the "County Government" listings in the blue pages of your telephone book.

DESIGNER CREDITS

Designers are listed sequentially. For clarification, the following position indicators may be used: Top (T), Middle (M), Bottom (B); Left (L), Right (R).

The Berger Partnership: 88 ML. **Julia Berman:** 20 BL; 31 TR. **Kurt Bluemel:** 3 TL; 4. **Tom Chakas/Roger Raiche:** 22 TR. **Chicago Botanic Garden:** 67 MR. **Bob Chittock:** 21 BR. **Bob Clark:** 21 TR; 23 BR; 33 BR; 45 L; 79 TL; 88 TR. **Denver Botanic Garden:** 34 TR; 51 TR. **Neil Diboll:** 15 BR; 67 B. **Marcia Donahue:** 65 BR. **Rachel Foster:** 52 BL. **Harland Hand:** 48 BL. **Kristin Horn:** 70 ML. **Chris Jacobson:** 79 BL. **Kelly House/Studio 6:** 89 BR. **Elizabeth Lair:** 53 TR. **Landcraft Environments** 50; 102 BL. **Ton Ter Linden:** 45 MR. **Longwood Gardens:** 63 BL. **Ann Lovejoy:** 20 BR; 52 T. **Ron Lutsko:** 25 BL. **Roberto Burle Marx:** 15 BL. **Ann Mehaffy:** 23 MR. **Jeff Mendoza/Barbara Toll:** 91 TL. **Carrie Nimmer:** 45 BR. **Juanita Nye:** 103 TR. **Marietta & Ernie O'Byrne:** 8 BL; 60 BR; 100 BL. **Oehme, van Sweden Assoc., Inc.:** 14 MR; 55 R; 70 BL; 80 BL, BR; 86 B; 87 BL; 94 TR; 96 B; 102 BR. **Michelle Osbourne:** 92 TR. **Piet Oudolf:** 15 T; 44 T; 63 T. **Judith Phillips:** 31 BR. **Planet Horticulture Design:** 1; 3 ML; 38; 40 T; 54 B. **Suzanne Porter:** 51 B; 59 TL; 93 T. **Roger Raiche:** 18 BR. **Chris Rosmini:** 35 R. **Michael Schultz:** 40 BL, BR; 49 BL. **Sally Shoemaker:** 3 TR; 16; 20 T. **Carol Shuler:** 65 T. **Jill Slater:** 106 TL, TR; 107 BR; 108 TL, BL; 109 TR. **Lauren Springer:** 72 BR. **Brad Stangeland:** 84 BL. **David Stevens/Julian Dowle:** 64 BR. **Sticky Wicket:** 94 MR. **Jane Sweetser:** 64 T. **Brandon Tyson:** 10 TR; 53 TL. **Tom Vetter:** 51 TL. **Edwina Von Gal:** 93 BR. **Ron Wagner/Nani Waddoups:** 13 BL. **Tom Wilhite:** 36 All; 37 All. **Geoffrey Whiten:** 92 BR. **Patrick Wynniatt-Husey/Patrick Clarke:** 64 BL.

ACKNOWLEDGMENTS

Our thanks to the following:

Steve Bender; Carol Bornstein; Stephen Breyer, Tripple Brook Farm, Southampton, MA; Jim Brockmeyer; Trevor Cole; Gib Cooper; Rick Darke; Neil Diboll; John Greenlee; Mary Hockenberry Meyer, University of Minnesota, St. Paul, MN; Rick Matthews, Madrone Landscaping, Atascadero, CA; Kit Morris and Garth Phillips; Thomas Leo Ogren; Roger Raiche, Berkeley, CA; David Salman, Santa Fe Greenhouses, Santa Fe, NM; John Schmidt, Toro Company; Jill Slater; Ron Smith, Cal Coast Irrigation, Paso Robles, CA; James S. Stolley, Jr.; Rick Storre, Freshwater Farms, Eureka, CA; Lambert Vrijmoed, Free Spirit Nursery, Langley, B.C.; Bill Uber, Van Ness Water Gardens, Upland, CA; Lance Walheim; Jennifer York.

INDEX

Only genera are included in the index. For species and common names, see pages 122-125. **Bold face** page numbers refer to photos.